M000305971

Gems from Bishop
Taylor Smith's Bible

Gems from Bishop
Taylor Smith's Bible

AMBASSADOR

BELFAST ◆ GREENVILLE
NORTHERN IRELAND   SOUTH CAROLINA

Gems from Bishop Taylor Smith's Bible

This edition 1997

ISBN   1 898787 92 1

AMBASSADOR PRODUCTIONS LTD,
Providence House
16 Hillview Avenue,
Belfast, BT5 6JR
Northern Ireland

Emerald House,
1 Chick Springs Road, Suite 206
Greenville,
South Carolina 29609
United States of America

FOREWORD

I WRITE with much pleasure, because the compiling of this volume has been undertaken that many of those, who during the life-time of Bishop Taylor Smith were blessed through his ministry, might be able to participate in and enjoy in some measure the treasures contained in his large wide-margin study Bible.

Unfortunately, it is impracticable to reproduce this Bible with its margins stored with condensed sermon outlines, biographical notes, and pithy sayings, many of which are gems sparkling with freshness and originality. With a view to bringing some of its treasures within the reach of many who held Bishop Taylor Smith in such high esteem and real affection, Mr. Ruoff has made a selection, and with considerable skill, grouped together under suggestive headings, some of these treasures.

The inclusion of a facsimile of a page from the Bishop's Bible, will be much appreciated, for a glance at this will give a true idea of the Bishop's orderly and concise notes which are so beautifully written in his clear and characteristic handwriting.

Very many of those who were privileged to meet and converse with the Bishop will recall how frequently, with his cheery greeting, he would ask, "What is your best thought this morning?" To some of those who did not know him well, and who perhaps did not happen to be aware of a "best thought," the question was somewhat embarrassing. Some of the Bishop's more intimate friends proved that the best line of defence was to attack, and before the Bishop got in his question they had asked him for his own " best thought." He was always prepared, and many a thought gem were they privileged to listen to from his lips. It was his practice each morning, during his quiet time for reading and prayer, to write down on a piece of paper his "best thought." He transcribed many of these into the margin of his Bible.

Some who read these pages may not come across any "best thought" which they have had the privilege of hearing from the Bishop's own lips, but all can be sure that they are reading many which he must have expressed from time to time.

Manifold and gracious are God's ways. May it please Him to use the written words of Bishop Taylor Smith now, as He used his spoken words while he was still with us.

J. M. WAITE.

PREFACE

BISHOP TAYLOR SMITH never wrote a book. But he left behind a legacy to the whole Church of God—his wide margin Bible.

In this Book he wrote down a great variety of his thoughts, in "picked and packed words" of rare quality, in beautiful handwriting. "Seed thoughts" was a phrase continually on the Bishop's lips. The margins of his Bible are crowded with such gems. To make a selection of these in a single book is to be confronted with *embarras de richesse.*

His spirituality, his humanity, his shrewdness, his humour, his mother wit, his sententious sayings, which were so characteristic of his public ministry and his private conversations, reappear in glowing word and vivid phrase in his Bible comments. His humour stirs the imagination, his homely characterizations cling like burrs. Who but the Bishop, for instance, could ever have thought of saying, in reference to the seraphic Isaiah (who had been describing in scathing terms the attire of the Daughters of Zion)— "The prophet must have had a peep into the ladies' wardrobes in Jerusalem"?; or again, his description of Saul, as "King and coward, tallest in height, shortest in courage"?; or of Rhoda, "rightly named Rhoda = Rose, for the perfume of her faith and confession and her appropriation of God's goodness scents the air to-day"?

The autobiographical note which so frequently appears in the Bishop's Bible, gives an insight into his inner life.

Sometimes it takes the form of a short fervent prayer, often the breathing of burning aspirations, always on the high level of fellowship with God and service for man. There is one very touching reference to Elijah's translation, foreshadowing his own—as *they still went on and talked* (these words are underlined). The marginal comment is, "Blessed call Home, in the midst of holy fellowship and intercourse." It was just in this way that the Bishop received his call Home. "As he sat at the breakfast table, he bowed his head again, and before he could lift it from his thanksgiving, he had gone."

In this book will be found sermons for preachers, valuable material for Christian missionaries and workers, choice sayings to be stored in the memory, a treasury of golden thoughts coming from the heart of a man of God, who one day remarked to the compiler of this book, "Heaven is more real to me than earth."

What were the secrets of Bishop Taylor Smith's influence, his personality, his serene poise? The answer can be discovered, in part, in the pages of his much-marked Bible, which reveal how constantly and deeply he drank of the streams of living water, and how intensely personal was his "fellowship with the Father and His Son."

It may certainly be said of the Bishop what Isaac Walton said of Dr. Sibbes, the Puritan,

"Of that blest man let this just praise be given,
Heaven was in him before he was in Heaven."

Perhaps the Bishop's true biography may be found amongst the pages of quotations which are written in this book.

PERCY O. RUOFF

Waltham Cross

CONTENTS

PART I

What the Bishop wrote about

PART II

The Bishop's Comments on

ix

CONTENTS

PART III

The Bishop's notes on

PART IV

The Bishop's

PART I

- Blessed Lord & Master.
- Behold Thy servant, by Thy Grace.
  - Search - Try - See - Lead.
  - Cleanse - Fill - Quite - Guard - Bless.
- Give a vision of Thyself :
  - Grant a realization of Thy Love & Power.
- Give a vision of Thy people & their needs.
    - Make me Thy messenger, &
channel of blessing before angels &
men - for Thy dear Name's sake .
                    Amen .

It was the Bishop's custom frequently to write a prayer for his
personal use. A prayer is here reproduced which the Bishop sent to
the Compiler of this volume on July 14th, 1936.

CHAPTER I

CHRIST

A SURVEY of Bishop Taylor Smith's references to the Son of God makes it evident that he wrote with profound reverence, worship and adoration. To him the Person of Christ was too great and excellent for detailed elaboration or prying examination. The Son surpasses knowledge ("No man knoweth the Son but the Father."—Matt. xi, 27); He evokes homage and allegiance. The Bishop's words are definite and straightforward, and touch those major phases of His manifestation, which exhibit His Eternal Godhead and His Manhood, bridging Heaven and earth. There is a wealth of spiritual teaching expressed in delicate thought. He writes these words, for example, about the Lord's boyhood: "Little are we told of our Lord's boyhood, reminding us of the silent building of the Temple." Or take the reference to Mary of Bethany, with very costly ointment of spikenard anointing the Lord: "How keen the insight of love to detect the true uses and ends of service." Then again, there is the charming reference to the doves on sale at the Temple, and the Lord's considera-tion that they might not fly away and be lost. The comment about the earthquake, "to let the earth see there was an empty tomb"; and the Resurrection, which "the Apostles dared not to have preached in Jerusalem if it had been a lie;" and His enthronement so that "the stream of power

comes from the enthroned Christ in Heaven and in us;"
all go to show that the Christian faith is founded upon
great facts.   How stimulating is the note: "You must
expect your risen Lord, not only in worship, but in work."
So also are the words: "Christ is as real (though invisible
to us) as He was to the disciples."

These are some of the Bishop's notes:—

His Centrality

The central fact in history is the manifestation of the
Son of God in the flesh.   "This is my beloved Son."
Christ was the only holy spot on which the Heavenly
Dove could rest.

Mark the first peal of thunder. "In the beginning"
(John).

His Greatness

His wisdom was the finest, His judgment the truest,
His analysis of life the deepest, His assertion of duty
the most authoritative that human ears have ever heard.
It needs distance to make a man look great.   God manifest
in the flesh alone can bear minute, penetrating inspection,
for He was holy.

It was the Name, the Person, which stirred the early
Church, and the same must stir the Church now.

His Boyhood

Little are we told of our Lord's boyhood, reminding
us of the silent building of the Temple.

His Poverty

Remember Christ was a poor man and no doubt often comes to us in the form of a poor man now.

His Comprehensiveness

Christ gathered up into Himself all that the holy men of God had written, and now He writes in our hearts. Christ only wrote once—in the sand (see John viii, 6).

His Love of Nature

Our Saviour was a keen observer of nature. Nature was to Him what it ought to be to us, the echo of the Father's voice.

His Insight

"Let her alone; against the day of my burying hath she kept this."—*John xii*, 7.

How keen the insight of love to detect the true uses and ends of service.

His Consideration

"And he said unto them that sold doves, Take these things hence."—*John ii*, 16.

See the consideration of our Lord that the doves might not fly away and be lost.

His Love

Love (1 Cor. xiii).   What love here does, Christ, who came to manifest God the Father, did; hence God is Love.

His Wide Mercy

"Send her away."—*Matt. xv*, 23.

What a contrast between Christ and His disciples.   Christ never sent away a single applicant.

His Appreciation of Faith

"O woman, great is thy faith."—*Matt. xv*, 28.

Christ did not say "Great is thy argument, patience, love," although they were great, but He seizes the mother grace from which all graces flow, viz. faith.

His Temptations

Christ's test of Sonship is obedience and entire trust in God, who alone is the giver of every good gift.   The Devil's test of Sonship is the supply of bodily wants, external prosperity, etc.   It is no sin to make stones into bread, but Christ received orders from God and not from the Devil.

His Tears

"He beheld the city, and wept over it."—*Luke xix*, 41.

The Saviour Christ saw the present with Eternity's eyes. Hence here the Divine and deepest pity exclaims the words "*If thou hadst known.*"

His Sorrows

"See if there be any sorrow like unto my sorrow."
—*Lam. i*, 12.

Not as the great painter Da Vinci has painted Christ, a man burdened with His own sorrows, but a sympathizing Christ who took the sorrows of others into his own heart.

"My God, my God, why hast thou forsaken me?"
—*Matt. xxvii*, 46.

This is hell.

His Abandonment

"And they all forsook him and fled."—*Mark xiv*, 50.

Sad to think only one young man befriended Christ, and he too ran away when the enemy became insolent. Many in Jerusalem would not forgo an hour's rest on His behalf that night—an opportunity run from is gone for ever.

His Answer to a Cry

"To-day shalt thou be with me in paradise."—
Luke xxiii, 43.

To Herod He had answered nothing. To Pilate's question "Whence art thou?" He made no reply; but to the penitent thief, "To-day . . . with Me."

His Empty Tomb

"And behold, there was a great earthquake."
—*Matt. xxviii*, 2.

This happened to let the earth see there was an empty tomb, and not to let the Lord out.

His Resurrection

"Whom God hath raised up."—*Acts ii*, 24.

The Apostles dared not to have preached this in Jerusalem if it had been a lie—besides the Holy Spirit could not have blessed a lie. Here is a proof of the Resurrection.

His Dominion

"I have heard thee in a time accepted."—2 *Cor. vi*, 2.

This work begins, not with the preacher, but with Christ, who asked for the nations, and laboured for them.

His Enthronement

"Therefore, being by the right hand of God exalted . . . He hath shed forth this."—*Acts ii*, 33.

The stream of power comes from the enthroned Christ in Heaven and in us.

His Bestowment

"Receive ye the Holy Ghost."—*John xx*, 22.

Here we have the gift of the Holy Spirit, as God breathed into Adam the "breath of life" so Christ breathed into His disciples His quickening Spirit.

His Ladder to Heaven

"Hereafter ye shall see heaven open."—*John i*, 51.

Acknowledge Christ as God's Son and your King and greater revelations shall be yours in the fellowship of the

Son of Man. Jacob's ladder is an abiding revelation—Christ is an immovable ladder set up on earth. Requests and answers are through Him.

The glory and power of Christ are ever manifested at man's extremity.

His Manifestation

"Jesus stood on the shore."—*John xxi*, 4.

You must expect your Risen Lord, not only in worship, but in work—"Lo, I am with you always." Obey Him as well as pray to Him. He lives to feed us with Himself. He cares for our temporal welfare.

His Gospel

As the Heavens into which He ascends overarch the whole world, so His Gospel takes a world-wide flight.

His Omnipresence

Christ is as real (though invisible to us) as He was to the disciples. The Teacher in the heart has His chair in Heaven.

His Body

Christ may be said to be without hands and lips. We, His saints, are His body, and as such, we serve to suffer with Him. The Church, the Body, is the organ of Christ's life and thought and will.

His Dedicated Way

"Having therefore, brethren, boldness to enter into the holiest by the blood of Jesus."—*Heb. x*, 19.

The way for us through the Veil is a living way. The work of Luther and Napoleon is linked to their history; the work of Jesus to His Person.

His Doctrine

Every development beyond the iimit of Christ's doctrine is a leap into the darkness, a supposed progress, but a retrocession—a ceasing to hold fast.

CHAPTER II

THE HOLY SCRIPTURES

AROUND the question of the inspiration of the Scriptures theological battles, fierce and long, have raged, and are still raging. There is a serene and uplifting presentation set forth with the language of experience, shown in the annexed quotations. Starting with the striking words (referring to the Scriptures) "Copyrighted in Heaven," they finish with the words "Inspiration is a miracle." The Old and New Testament are alike appealed to as God's Word. In more than one casual sentence can be found illuminating matter which confirms the belief that in the Holy Scriptures men possess "the living oracles," "God-breathed." A stroke from the Bishop's pen on some unfamiliar Scriptures illuminates the theme, and gives, not proof, but evidence of the origin and prescience of the Word of God.

"Many read, few feed." On the flyleaf of his Bible the Bishop has a variation of these words. He writes, "Not only read, but feed," and against this observation there is a neatly drawn index finger pointing to the words, as if to indicate that above other considerations the grace of meditation stands first.

The paragraph beginning "Man shall not live by bread alone" expounds this thought cogently and is worthy of continual reference.

Copyrighted in Heaven

"For ever, O Lord, thy word is settled in heaven."—*Ps. cxix*, 89.

The Bible may be disputed here by many, but it is copyrighted in Heaven.

Meditate!

"This book of the law . . . meditate therein day and night."
—*Joshua i*, 8.

It seems a small book for such an amount of labour and study, yet God's word is "meditate," and I say Amen.

Inspiration of Holy Scriptures

". . . . There is bdellium and the onyx stone."—*Gen. ii*, 12.

Even the names of the gems are given to show the chapter is no fable.

"The Lord said in his heart."—*Gen. viii*, 21.

Without inspiration how could this be?

The Book of Esther

Why is God's name omitted? A heathen country, hence a heathen book brimful of God's care of His people. (God is mentioned in the Septuagint, Chapter II, 20.) Esther is like the Holy of Holies, left empty, to show the presence of One who fills all space. The interposition of Providence as seen in Esther, is proof that God is with

His people wherever they may be, dispersed as now, after the Captivity.

". . . To take the spoil of them for a prey."—*Esther iii*, 13.

Without the Old Testament history regarding Amalek these words would be meaningless. Marvellous coincidence of the genuineness of the book. Although the Assyrian king gave leave to take spoil, God never allowed the spoil of Amalek to be touched.

Mordecai's Faith

"For if thou altogether holdest thy peace at this time, then shall there enlargement and deliverance arise to the Jews from another place."—*Esther iv*, 14.

Don't tell me this book is a story of Eastern origin if there is no mention of God in it. Where do you find such faith as Mordecai's in the promise to Abraham that God would interfere and give the Jews deliverance?

God's Perfect Way

"As for God, his way is perfect."—*Ps. xviii*, 30.

We cannot add to a perfect thing. To meddle is to spoil.

Kingdoms and the Kingdom of God

"Fear not, *little flock;* for it is your Father's good pleasure to give you the kingdom."—*Luke xii*, 32.

Little flock! Sweet expression.

All other kingdoms shall fall like: (1) a pack of cards, (2) a sand-castle, (3) snow before the sun.

Realities Exceed Types

The rich man and Lazarus. Luke xvi. This is a proof of eternal woe, for realities always exceed types, and our Lord, who alone can see before and behind, preached it.

A Minimum Obligation

"O how love I thy law ! It is my meditation all the day."
—*Ps. cxix*, 97.

It is as little as we can do to read our Bibles when we think of those who had the trouble of translation.

A Triple Ministry

"When thou goest, it shall lead thee; when thou sleepest, it shall keep thee; and when thou awakest, it shall talk with thee."—*Prov. vi*, 22.

God's law to help when conscious, unconscious, and semi-conscious.

It is our duty to enquire and search for that which we do not understand.

Four Gospels, Four Pictures

The four Gospels, though flowing from one Paradise, go forth to water the earth with four currents of different volume and direction. The four Gospels are also like four varied pictures of our Lord, painted by four loving hands, each picture disclosing fresh beauties.

A Notable Omission

In the genealogy in Matthew, mark the absence of those who died by the visitation of God or man—Ahaziah, Athaliah, Joash, Amaziah.

The Abiding Star

"When they saw the star, they rejoiced with exceeding great joy."—*Matt. ii*, 10.

And so the star remains, for whenever Christ is sought in His Word the Holy Spirit points to Christ, and exceeding great joy follows.

Many Read, Few Feed

"Man shall not live by bread alone, but by every word that proceedeth out of the mouth of God."—*Matt. iv*, 4.

If we want to be fat and flourishing we must feed much on God's Word. Many read, few feed. The Bible is silent to the careless, but to the digger rich. You cannot be noble unless you love your Bible (Acts xvii, 11).

An Unfinished Record

The book of the Acts of the Apostles is unfinished to teach us that we have a page to add, ere Christ comes.

The Promises

"For all the promises of God in him are yea, and in him Amen."—*2 Cor. i*, 20.

Subject to no discount.

Inspiration—a Miracle

"All scripture is given by inspiration of God."
—2 *Tim. iii*, 16.

Inspiration is a miracle, and cannot be explained. I do not understand how a few loaves could be made to feed five thousand.

CHAPTER III

THERE is a fragrance and exquisite charm, reminiscent of the Bishop's singular ministry, which is quickly detected in the jottings contained in this section. The imagery and refinement which are employed to picture the deeper experiences of the Christian life are all so characteristic of this gracious man. Who is likely to forget such sentences as these: "Only in quiet waters can we see the reflection of His face." "The way to be taught—silent, sitting." "Trust neither the low nor high: go higher." "It is from daily manna, heroes are made." "These two, east and west, can never be brought together, so our sins and us when once forgiven." And: "To Africa? To pulpit? Yes, and anywhere else."

"The Psalmist's experience is like camomile—sweetest when crushed." These comments on the Psalms yield a sweetness which will refresh many a weary traveller on life's highway, and be as healing medicine to those who are spiritually run down. It is indeed a privilege to go to the familiar Book of Psalms and to sit at the feet of a qualified teacher of spiritual truth.

Crushed Camomile

The Psalmist's experience is a broken one, like camomile—sweetest when crushed.

27

The Ministry of Still Waters

"He leadeth me beside the still waters."—*Ps. xxiii*, 2.

Only in quiet waters can we see the reflection of His face.

A Noble Inscription

"The earth is the Lord's."—*Ps. xxiv*, 1.

The late Prince Consort, viewing the Royal Exchange said, "One thing is lacking, viz. an acknowledgement of God." Then he was asked to choose some words and he chose the above.

The Scholar's Attitude

"Teach me thy way, O Lord. . . . Wait on the Lord."
—*Ps. xxvii*, 11 and 14.

The way to be taught—silent, sitting.

An Overflowing Heart

Psalm xlv. To the chief musician upon (1) Shoshannim, (2) for the sons of Korah, (3) Maschil, a song of loves.

(1) The title Shoshannim—upon lilies, (2) God's songs require good singers, (3) they instruct indeed. Such love must boil over.

"Thou art fairer than the children of men; grace is poured into thy lips."—*Ps. xlv*, 2.

In Person, mind, character, beauty and eloquence make a man majestic.

Weary, but Resting

Psalm lv. Title. The Righteous One's weary soul resting on the certainty of what the Lord will do.

The Gladdening River

"There is a river, the streams whereof shall make glad the city of God."—*Ps. xlvi*, 4.

More peace and joy (tranquillity), is to be derived from the trickling stream of God's help in the City than from the mighty waters of the world.

"There is a river" (grace); its streams are the blood of Jesus, the influence of the Holy Spirit, the promises of the Word of God, the means of grace. There are four ways in which the stream of a river gladdens the citizen: (1) as a means of beauty, a city's beauty depends on its river, (2) as a means of traffic (wealth). What would London be without the Thames? (3) As regards fertility. Imagine a dry and thirsty land in which no water is. Such is the godless man—no fruit. What a contrast to "much fruit." (4) Water supply. What could a city do without water—a besieged city—water cut off—soon surrendered. Ours can never be cut off, praise the Lord. The enemy may sit for ever. Our supplies are eternal. "Whoso drinketh of the water that I shall give him shall never thirst."

The Tenderness of God

"Thou tellest my wanderings; put thou my tears into thy bottle."—*Ps. lvi*, 8.

As though God followed and preserved every sigh and tear.

Go Higher!

"Trust in Him at all times. . . . Surely men of low degree are vanity, and men of high degree are a lie."—*Ps. lxii*, 8 and 9.

Trust neither the low nor high: go higher.

A Visit to the Sanctuary

"Until I went into the sanctuary of God."—*Ps. lxxiii*, 17.

Here indeed many difficulties are made plain.

The Gift of a Day

"The day is thine."—*Ps. lxxiv*, 16.

Each day a special gift from God—use it well.

Wilderness Provision

"Can God furnish a table in the wilderness?"—*Ps. lxxviii*, 19.

Yes indeed He can, and a good one too. It is from daily manna that heroes are made.

For Character Building

"Thou hast lifted me up and cast me down."—*Ps. cii*, 10.

Both are necessary for the perfecting of character: winter and summer, sunshine and shower: prosperity and adversity.

The Monte Rosa of the Psalms

"Bless the Lord, O my soul."—*Ps. ciii*, 1.

Soul music is the best after all and beats even Nebuchadnezzar's band in Dan. iii, 5.

". . . thy youth is renewed like the eagles !"—Verse 5.

Christians are called to be young eagles, ever on the wing (keen-sighted for God's glory and man's welfare), not young owls (ever moping).

"As far as the east is from the west, so far hath he removed our transgressions from us."—Verse 12.

These two, east and west, can never be brought together, so our sins and us when once forgiven.

An Hundredfold, and——

"And he brought forth his people with joy and his chosen with gladness: and gave them the lands of the heathen."—
Ps. cv, 43, 44.

Do I see the degrees of Christians here? Yes, dear Lord. An hundredfold in this world, and what in the world to come?

Great Waters or Shallow Waters

"They that go down to the sea in ships, that do business in great waters. These see the works of the Lord, and his wonders in the deep."—*Ps. cvii*, 23, 24.

Why do we shrink from great waters—without them we cannot see great wonders. Shallow water Christians see but few wonders.

An Encompassing Providence

"The Lord shall preserve *thy going out and thy coming in* from this time forth and even for evermore."—*Ps. cxxi*, 8.

To Africa? To pulpit? Yes, and anywhere else.

How Firm a Foundation!

"Many a time have they afflicted me from my youth, may Israel now say."—*Ps. cxxix*, 1.

The enemies of God try to wear out the saints of the Most High, but they are strong, having built on the Rock.

CHAPTER IV

BIBLE CHARACTERS

IT has pleased God to employ biography in the Holy Scriptures to teach important lessons. The lives of men and women, with a true and unbiased record of their failures and successes, their fears and hopes, their struggles and victories, their ambitions and attainments, and their sorrows and joys (for this is what the Bible gives), are, for reasons which are apparent, a form of teaching which affords at once impetus and warning. Those who listened to Bishop Taylor Smith when he referred to Bible characters will recall the fact that his life-like sketches gave fresh insight into their characters. Fortunately, his Bible holds many references which will be recognized as having been introduced into his public addresses, and many more which have evidently been written for private use. How sagacious, for example, is the Bishop's comment about Abraham—and applicable to all—"Each saint is seen to fall in the very grace for which he is most noted." And the words: "Though we may not complain *of,* yet we may complain *to* God"—the first showing a reaction which virtually judges the "right wiseness" of God; the second is the expression of his feelings such as Asaph gave (Ps. lxxiii) when, smarting under the pressure of life, he honestly complained: "*My heart and my flesh faileth,* but God is the strength of my heart and my portion for ever."

ABRAHAM

Abram's Call

"Now the Lord had said unto Abram, Get thee out of thy country, and from thy kindred and from thy father's house. . . ."—*Gen. xii*, 1.

A beautiful illustration of personal connection—God calling us to be His friends. To all such who respond, He is shield and reward. . . . Age, position, prospects are nothing to the man of God, all are counted loss for Christ. . . . Oh for steadfastness of purpose, faith and obedience, eh ?

What a fool Abraham must have appeared to his worldly relatives ! He could not see the One who called him and they did not believe in Him.

"Who teacheth like Him ? "

"And Abram passed through . . . unto the plain of Moreh."—*Gen. xii*, 6.

Moreh, the place of teaching. The Canaanite was in the land. It is the Lord who teacheth my fingers to fight.

Altars

"There builded he an altar unto the Lord who appeared unto him . . and there he builded an altar."—*Gen. xii*, 7, 8.

These prepared him for his great sacrifice.

Carnal Policy

"Say, I pray thee, thou art my sister."—*Gen. xii*, 13.

Carnal policy never pays. Mark the candour of Scripture. Its heroes are not glossed over. Each saint is seen to fall in the very grace for which he is most noted—Abraham, faith ; Moses, meekness, etc. Who walks by faith in God walks surely, who walks by sight falls. Who does not reprove the world must be reproved by the world.

At every stage Abraham prayed. May every stray pilgrim get back to Bethel where the last altar stands.

Refusal and Reward

"I will not take from a thread even to a shoe latchet."
—*Gen. xiv*, 23.

Immediately after Abraham refused these worldly rewards, we read that God promised to be his reward (abundant). After victory (a good thing) God comes and says, I have better things in store. Where there is great faith, there may be many fears (2 Cor. vii, 5).

Legitimate and Sinful Complaint

"And Abram said, Lord God, what wilt thou give me, seeing I go childless."—*Gen. xv*, 2.

Though we may not complain *of*, yet we may complain *to* God.

ISHMAEL

The Arab

Gen. xvi, 15. The Arab, so troublesome, was the result of impatience.

MOSES

In the paragraphs which follow will be found *multum in parvo*. How weighty are the words on Moses' education and training: "The man whom God educates is educated, and none other." In the Heavenly School God is the teacher, and all who would teach spiritual lessons must first sit as pupils in this school. Mr. Spurgeon wrote: "I would to God that my readers were all entered as diligent scholars in Jesus' College, students of Corpus Christi, or the body of Christ, resolved to attain unto a good degree in the learning of the cross." The Bishop adds: "Our Lord spent ten times the time in private to that in public." The paragraphs "Unhurried Training" and "The Discipline of the Desert" are two priceless (in the truest sense) paragraphs—the one, in well-selected words, calling for patient endurance in the period of training, the other (again in beautiful language) showing with great clearness that the place of vision and the place of Heavenly lore is the Divine Presence. These thoughts cannot be too often or too thoroughly considered. There are other shining "gems" which need no indication.

Educated by God

A man who ventures on a public career without a training is like a ship going to sea without ballast. The man whom God educates is educated, and none other. God only can make a man a vessel fit for the Master's use. Human wisdom at its best can never constitute a servant of God. Think of Moses at Horeb, Elijah at Cherith, Ezekiel at Chebar, Paul in Arabia, John in Patmos. Our Lord spent ten times the time in private to that in public.

Unthought-of Potentialities

Noah made an ark, and Moses' mother an ark of bulrushes that death might not swallow her child. Who thought that the small babe would one day shake Egypt!

Unhurried Training

God never hurries over the training of His servants. It took forty years to find out how strong he was, and another forty ere he knew his own weakness and God's grace to be sufficient for him and his life work. You cannot educate a natural man into a spiritual one. If so, Moses might have been so, for he was grown, educated, and mighty in word and deed.

Looking Both Ways

"And he (Moses) looked this way and that way."—*Exod. ii*, 12.

When a man looks this way and that way he is not fit to be a deliverer. Had he seen a man: what then? The man who looks up and sees God cannot see man.

The Discipline of the Desert

What a trial (the desert) for a man strong in body and mind! What a change of circumstances—a learned man and shepherd. Things are rightly valued at the backside of the desert—din and bustle are not heard there, ambition has no range. We see things in the stillness of the Divine presence. To learn *of* God we must be *with* Him. It is no waste of time. A man who is always doing, is apt to do too much.

Training in Obedience

"And the Lord said unto Moses, Put forth thine hand, and take it by the tail."—*Exod. iv*, 4.

God will manifest His powers to His servants. Here

Moses is taught obedience, for it is contrary to all experience to handle serpents thus.

A Reed or a Rock

"And the Lord said unto him, What is that in thine hand? And he said, A rod."—*Exod. iv*, 2.

Man will trust a reed that can be seen, rather than the unseen Rock of Ages.

Who dares Excuse when God says I AM?

"I am slow of speech."—*Exod. iv*, 10.

Who dares say I am slow, when God says, I am *with?* Whatever is necessary may be set over against I AM. When God is with our infirmity it only offers greater opportunities for the display of His power. Paul said, "I take pleasure in infirmities," a wonderful experience (2 Cor. xii, 9, 10).

Moses cast away the high calling, and Aaron shared the glory. Not humility, but unbelief (pride) prevented him. What can eloquence do that God cannot do? Let me be rather a divine stammerer than a human orator. Reliance on God is the secret of power. The person whose presence we deem essential to our progress often proves a hindrance rather than a help.

CALEB

Caleb Reviews his Life

Caleb, a man who wholly followed God, is mentioned six times. See how he strengthens his faith by reviewing his life, "And now, behold, the Lord hath kept me alive, as he said." Who lives with God is ever strong, "As yet I am as strong this day as I was in the day that Moses sent me" (Josh. xiv, 10, 11.) As Joshua blessed Caleb, so Jesus will bless us. Caleb at eighty-five years claims the promised inheritance, yes, and enters on possession. It was a wonderful faith in God's power, for the Anakims were there. God's Presence, not Caleb's, was to do the driving out.

GIDEON

Starting at Home

Gideon's work had to begin at home. When we are in earnest those we fear most are on our side.

A Peril Averted

"And the Lord said unto Gideon, The people are yet too many."—*Judges vii*, 4.

Gideon would have taken the praise probably.

Confidence Assured

"Arise, get thee down unto the host, for I have delivered it into thine hand."—*Judges vii*, 9.

God gives us confidence before leading us to victory.

If God be for Us

"Lo, a cake of barley bread tumbled into the host of Midian."—*Judges vii*, 13.

The coarsest, cheapest, humblest kind of food—thus teaching Gideon and us that "If God be for us, who can be against us?"

Typical Victories

"The sword of the Lord and of Gideon."—*Judges vii*, 20.

Typical of our victories by preaching the everlasting Gospel and holding forth the light given.

SAMSON

How God Refreshes His Servants

"But God clave a hollow place that was in the jaw."
—*Judges xv*, 19.

Samson's weapon a source of refreshment. After fighting with our jawbone and becoming weary and thirsty, the Lord cleaves a hollow—a text, a promise, and sends forth refreshing streams.

CHAPTER V

BIBLE CHARACTERS (*Continued*)

DAVID

AMONGST the shrewd and balanced notes, there are two choice sayings. The first, "David's recreation on the hills of Bethlehem became his strength in the day of adversity." All life affecting the spirit, soul and body may be related to the will of God. John Smith (a remarkable master at Harrow some eighty years ago) used to say that he kept his body fit as part of his consecration to God.

"David was not ashamed to feed sheep after court life." It may well be asked, Does anything (but sin) degrade a man, if done in obedience to the Will of God?

The five smooth stones from the brook: "(1) God is, (2) God has, (3) God can, (4) God will, (5) God does," will be greatly serviceable to Christians in fighting any ancient or modern giants, and if these stones are "embedded in the sling of faith, and slung with a strong arm" they will bring down a Goliath or any of his numerous descendants.

David's Victories—Recreation Turned to Good Account

None but a strong character would risk his life for a lamb.

David had three victories in one day: (1) over self when he overcame envy and anger, (2) over the world when he overcame the precautions of unbelief, and (3) over the Devil when he overcame the blaspheming giant Goliath. (See 1 Sam. xvii, 28, 33, 49.) Count no work common or unclean. David's recreation on the hills of Bethlehem became his strength in the day of adversity. To contemplate Goliath is to fear. To look unto God is to be saved.

Court Life, then Shepherding

David was not ashamed to feed sheep after court life. Our Father wants neither position nor possession, but submission. There is a greater victory than over Goliath —self-control, self-victory. Whatever we do, let us do it with our might—even slinging stones.

Five Smooth Stones against Giants

God wants us to use just what we have and what He has given us, in fighting our enemies. There are five smooth stones from the brook; (1) God is, (2) God has, (3) God can, (4) God will, (5) God does. Each stone should be embedded in the sling of faith, and slung with a strong arm.

We may be youths with sticks and stones at our disposal, but "It will be eno' if in the Name we go."

Where do we take our giants' heads, to Bethlehem? Jerusalem is the place.

David's Humility

"David answered, I am the son of thy servant Jesse."
—1 *Sam. xvii*, 58.

Humility crowns the day. God did it: I am but His servant and thine.

David was in no hurry to be king; he waited God's time for promotion.

SAMUEL

Youthful Service

"But Samuel ministered before the Lord, being a child."
1 *Sam. ii*, 18.

He served before he was converted.

A Highway to Service

"And the child Samuel grew on and was in favour both with the Lord and also with man."—1 *Sam. ii*, 26.

It is no sin to be in favour, but a highway to a large field of service.

If Spoken for Him

"And Samuel grew and the Lord was with him, and did let none of his words fall to the ground."—1 *Sam. iii*, 19.

So shall the Lord do for our words, if boldly spoken for Him. Everybody will hear if we are faithful to God, sooner or later it shall be declared.

JONAH

A Noble and Fearless Man

Jonah is a fearless man, not running away from his mission; fearing the Ninevites but hating the mission as seen by his after-conduct—probably jealous of God's mercy to the Gentiles. It is a wonderful book whether considered as historical or allegorical, for that a Jew should so write of God's compassion for a heathen city. Jonah was a noble man in writing thus the history of his sin—such conduct manifests true repentance.

Jonah forgot evidently his dignity and duty, in herding with passengers and mariners instead of being separate.

Throw the Old Adam Overboard

"The mariners . . . cast forth the wares that were in the ship into the sea."—*Jonah i, 5.*

The cargo, like the sins of a man, not the cause of the storm of God's wrath. It is the old Adam (nature) which must be thrown overboard, before peace is given and the heavenly shore reached.

Reproving or Reproved

He (Jonah) who ought to have been reproving is reproved. When we are inconsistent how insolent the enemy becomes.

Afterwards

"I know that for my sake this great tempest is upon you."
—*Jonah i,* 12.

No doubt Jonah praised God for this storm in after-life.

Human Nature

"But it displeased Jonah exceedingly, and he was very angry."—*Jonah iv*, 1.

Alas ! poor human nature !

SAUL

The Penalty of Walking by Sight

"And Saul said, Bring hither a burnt offering to me."
—1 *Sam. xiii*, 9.

Walking by sight and not by faith never paid.

"And Saul said, Because I saw that the people were scattered from me."—1 *Sam. xiii*, 11.

Often we, like Saul, walk by sight and lose our Kingdom thereby.

Saul's Failures

"And Saul said unto Ahiah, Bring hither the ark of God."
—1 *Sam. xiv*, 18.

Poor timid superstitious Saul.   Not time to trust and get strong.

"And Saul smote the Amalekites."—1 *Sam. xv*, 7.

He began well: but alas !

This Bleating

"And Samuel said, What meaneth then this bleating of the sheep in mine ears, and the lowing of the oxen which I hear ?"
—1 *Sam. xv*, 14.

Many, like Saul, boast of obedience to God, but what means then this indulgence of the flesh, their love of the world, their unkind spirit, their neglect of holy duties ?

Invalid Confession

"But the people took of the spoil."—1 *Sam. xv*, 21.

Confession of faults is not true when mixed with excuses.

The Cost of Surrender

"Behold, to obey is better than sacrifices."—1 *Sam. xv*, 22.

It is easier to bring a lamb than the will to God, eh?

Costly Failure

"And as Samuel turned about to go away, he laid hold upon the skirt of his mantle. . . ."—1 *Sam. xv*, 27.

If Saul had sought God's favour as he did Samuel's, it would have been better for him.

Appalling Deterioration

"And Samuel said, How can I go? If Saul hear it, he will kill me."—1 *Sam. xvi*, 2.

How bad Saul must have become for Samuel to think this.

DANIEL, AND THE THREE YOUNG MEN

The cameos of Daniel and the three young men are picturesque and beautifully executed, and will be read with much interest. The little bit about the etiquette of Heaven and Daniel's character at College are delightful. Some of the Bishop's sententious sayings might be classed as proverbs. For example: "A young man's profit consists not in what he receives, but in what he learns to forgo," and: "The highest elements in character require the subjugation of the appetites."

"The furnace was passed when the young men said
'No'." This last is a literary gem which enshrines a moral
crisis.

Still another proverbial saying: "Better be cast into
a den of lions than carry the lion of a bad conscience
within to tear you continually." What powerful imagery—
carrying a lion within! Shakespeare puts into the mouth
of Macbeth the words:

> "Canst thou not minister to a mind diseased,
> Pluck from the memory a rooted sorrow,
> Raze out the written troubles of the brain
> And with some sweet oblivious antidote
> Cleanse the stuff'd bosom of that perilous stuff
> Which weighs upon the heart?"

Perilous stuff, indeed, which weighs upon the heart. But
a lion, fierce, relentless, gripping his victim—a lion within
to tear continually!

"If we take care of God's glory, He will take care of
the very threads of our coats." What microscopic provi-
dences, recalling the saying of Christ: "The hairs of your
head are all numbered."

A Purpose which Dominated

"But Daniel purposed in his heart that he would not defile
himself with the portion of the King's meat."—*Dan. i*, 8.
The purpose of his heart became the subject of his words
and the practice of his life.

The Etiquette of Heaven

God will not suffer us to be tempted above our ability,
e.g. Job, Abraham, Daniel.

Daniel was placed in a very trying position. It would seem that everything depended on pleasing the king. Daniel felt that the thing of supreme importance was to please Jehovah. He believed God had power over idolatrous kings. A young man's profit consists not in what he receives, but in what he learns to forgo. The highest elements in character require the subjugation of the appetites. Kings' servants must have kings' food, and be prepared to stand in their presence. The etiquette of Heaven we learn here. Those who would excel in wisdom and piety must learn betimes to keep the body under. At College Daniel was remarkable for two things: (1) Godliness, (2) learning. He must have been well trained. . . . Wisdom is not confined to old age.

No Exemption from Trouble

"Nebuchadnezzar . . . his spirit was troubled."—*Dan. ii*, 1.

Kings are not exempt from trouble. Many live in pain as well as pomp.

Prayer First

"That they would desire mercies of the God of heaven."
—*Dan. ii*, 18.

His first step, prayer. God's people are not without trial, nor without God in the trial.

Another King's Voice Prevails

Chapter III. A picture of the world and its demands. Unrighteous in its demands, cruel in its commands. Evidently God's servants were obedient in coming. Another King's voice said, "Thou shalt not bow——"

No doubt many bowed for self or family advancement. The furnace was passed when the young men said "No." The executioner's death gave vacancies for God's three. The work of Daniel is one grand picture of manly nobility— of what young men have to undergo if they will serve God faithfully, of what *we* must do if God is to be magnified in us. Only confidence in God will save from and in death. It is sweet to fall down "bound," thrown by the world, if Christ catches us.

God Takes Care of His Own

"Lo, I see four men loose, walking in the midst of the fire."—*Dan. iii,* 25.

Christ lifted them up and comforted them with His presence. Troubles mean enrichment. When thrown in, don't be in too great a hurry to get out. If we take care of God's glory, He will take care of the very threads of our coats.

"Blessed be the God of Shadrach, Meshach, and Abednego, who hath sent his angel."—*Dan. iii,* 28.

How often God sends His angel, but who shall lift up those cast into the furnace, and who shall deliver from, or change, our King's word?

The Lion of a Bad Conscience

In the lion's den. Better be cast into a den of lions than carry the lion of a bad conscience within to tear you continually. Have you asked God to keep you safe from the roaring lion, the Devil? God does not kill the lions, but restrains them to make us keep on trusting. The best way to have a good night is to have a good conscience.

Kneeling First

"And behold, an hand touched me which set me upon my knees."—*Dan. x*, 10.

How necessary that the Lord should thus deal with us! We must kneel before we can stand upright.

PAUL

Paul's Eye on the Goal

Paul ever had his eye on the future welfare of his converts, not content with justification, he desired sanctification to follow.

The Fruit of Paul's Infirmity

"Ye know how through infirmity of the flesh I preached the gospel unto you at the first."—*Gal. iv*, 13.

All things work together for good. If Paul had not been hindered by a thorn in the flesh, the Galatians would not probably have heard the Gospel.

Paul's Gratitude

"I thank my God upon every remembrance of you."
—*Phil. i*, 3.

Mark Paul's gratitude for good men expressed in prayer.

Paul's Estimate of Himself and Christ

Paul longed to preach the Gospel at Rome. Persecution sent him a free passage, and gave him the cream of audiences. What became of Paul was nothing to him, but what the world would think of Christ was all in all. History has few stranger contrasts than when it shows us Paul preaching Christ under the walls of Nero's palace, the abyss of all crime and infamy.

Gazing on the Redeemer

"Who is the image of the invisible God."—*Col. i*, 15.

Paul seems to pass through the porch of Redemption to gaze on the Redeemer. May we. Those who have most of the image will have most of the dominion.

MARY MAGDALENE

Devotedness

"The first day of the week cometh Mary Magdalene early."—*John xx*, 1.

Grateful and faithful—last to leave the cross and first to come to the tomb.

RHODA

A Perpetual Aroma

"And as Peter knocked at the door of the gate, a damsel came to hearken named Rhoda."—*Acts xii*, 13.

Rightly named Rhoda=Rose, for the perfume of her faith and confession and her appropriation of God's goodness scents the air to-day.

CHAPTER VI

THERE are not many notes inscribed in Bishop Taylor Smith's Bible which specifically centre on this subject, but the principal references are appended. The opening paragraph presents a thrilling transition which is so worded as to stir the heart. "Last night," says this man of God, "they lay down to rest in the house of bondage, and their bodies securely slept under the blood. Then came the clear, blue sky and the song of salvation, 'Unto Him who sitteth upon the throne, and unto the Lamb'." What rapturous prospect! Last night. . . . Then. . . .

For those who are prepared to leave the barren and arid fields of controversy, and rest mind and heart on the *Lord* who is coming rather than on the *coming* of the Lord, who, in "that bright and golden morning" will say "Come and dine," there is power to purify the life, as the hope is "set on Him."

They Lay Down to Rest. Then . . . .

The exodus of our bodies is still future, and belongs to the Feast of Tabernacles yet to come. Of us, as of Israel, it shall be said, Last night they lay down to rest in the house of bondage, and their bodies securely slept under the blood. Then came the clear blue sky and the song of salvation, "unto Him who sitteth upon the throne, and unto the Lamb" beyond the reach of slavery.

An Illustration

The union of Christ and the Church will take place in perilous times, and in the morning as Exodus xiv, 24. Christ's second coming is illustrated by His coming in the fourth watch, walking on the sea.

Calamity Follows

Isaiah xxiv. In this 24th chapter we have a view of the calamity which will befall those left when the saints have been taken up to meet their Lord—all treated alike then. The conclusion of the chapter shows the Lord of hosts reigning in Zion.

The Birth Pangs

Ezekiel vii. As persecutions were the birth pangs which ushered in the Gentile Church, may not the tribulations here refer to the birth pangs which shall come when saints are withdrawn, and usher in the Jewish Church.

Look Up

"And when these things begin to come to pass, then look up."—*Luke xxi*, 28.

As in a railway cutting, the only beauty is above.

Come and Dine

John xxi. This chapter as Revelation xxii most assuredly
points to *the morning* when He, our Saviour, will appear,
and say, Come and dine (v. 12).
Christ's coming with His saints shows no separation
(see Rom. viii, 35).

Many do not Wait

"Ye turned to God from idols, to serve the living and true
God, and to wait for his Son from Heaven."—1*Thess. i*, 9, 10.

Alas, how many turn from idols, but don't go on to wait
for His Son from Heaven. Christ may come any day, so
let us be ready every day.

Diligence Rewarded

"Be diligent that ye may be found of him in peace."
—2 *Peter iii*, 14.

Only the diligent servant will be happy when the Lord
comes.

At the Close of Both Canons

It is remarkable that both canons close with the promise
of Christ's coming.

PART II

CHAPTER I

COMMUNION WITH GOD

THE marginal notes which have been collected and arranged under this heading have one or two autobiographical touches—notably the first note and the one on preaching. Confined mostly to words of one syllable, the Bishop says: "Who talks with God *often* and *long* shall also shine in face and deed. May I. Amen. . . . So may I talk to bring the people near." Not many Christians perhaps can tell of "talks with God often and long." Mr. Spurgeon once said in a public prayer which was reported: "May we, everyone, have an audience with God. To some of us Thou hast long been sweetly familiar; we have spoken more to Thee than with any other individual."[1] Another seraphic spirit, Charles A. Fox, wrote: "It is this holy waiting alone that gives the soaring spirit of vision and the eagle wings of ascension. . . . So souls that will catch the divine features, and perfect the divine image, and learn the divine accent, must study stillness, for only still waters give back the true reflection of earth or sky, and must live much in the company of the Invisible, and listen long and drink deep into His Spirit, often tarrying till dusk in the Temple of His Presence. . . ." One more witness may be cited. George

[1]*Behold the Throne of Grace*, p. 74. C. H. Spurgeon's prayers and hymns. Selected and arranged by Chas. T. Cook, Marshall, Morgan & Scott Ltd. 2s. 6d.

Müller said: "I saw more clearly than ever, that the first great and primary business, to which I ought to attend every day, was to have my soul happy in the Lord."[1]

Those who were brought into close touch with Bishop Taylor Smith would readily acknowledge that the words taken from his Bible, quoted above, were illustrated by his life.

The reference to the gift of grace to preach, shows how he magnified his office as a preacher of the Word of God.

The fresh and rich treatment of this subject will surely stir the hearts of Christian readers to a closer walk with God and create aspirations after making life "one unbroken thanksgiving." May the recorded words be as summonses to communion with God.

Communing with God Transfigures

"Moses wist not that the skin of his face shone while he talked with him . . . and they were afraid to come nigh him."—*Exod. xxxiv*, 29, 30.

Who talks with God often and long shall also shine in face and deed. May I. Amen.

And still people fear to approach: the Gospel is too good to be true. Moses had to talk to get them near— they feared death. So may I talk to bring the people near.

All who through grace are brought to commune with God confess "the half was never told." Communion with God transfigures the mind and body.

[1] *The Lord's Dealings with George Müller*, Vol. 1, pp. 404/405s.

Early Rising

"Those that seek me early shall find me."—*Prov. viii*, 17.

What an encouragement to rise up early. So the daily manna of God's word comes upon the dew of the Holy Spirit.

The Rock once smitten now must be spoken to. So to our Rock let us speak when the water seems scarce.

Perennial Springs

"Whosoever drinketh of the water that I shall give him shall never thirst."—*John iv*. 14.

Even earth's best and deepest well satisfies not. Oh for the well of Truth which neither freezes in winter nor disappears in summer.

Spiritual Worship

"God is a Spirit and they that worship him must worship him in spirit and in truth."—*John iv*, 24.

Place, form, manner, hour—all are nothing. Communion and contact of our spirit with the Spirit of God everything.

God's presence does not always bring life joy and peace, except to those who love Him.

Recognizing the Master

"Therefore that disciple whom Jesus loved saith unto Peter, It is the Lord."—*John xxi*, 7.

It is the disciple whom Jesus loves and who lives near to Him, who first recognizes the Master. This is ever the exclamation when blessings abound and power is manifested.

The True Order

"Jesus saith unto them, Come and dine."—*John xxi*, 12.

We must first dine before we can go and feed others.

A Lofty Aspiration

"That God may be all in all."—1 *Cor. xv*, 28.

At all times and in all places. Amen.

The Living Hope

"Christ in you, the hope of glory."—*Col. i*, 27.

A living hope, living in death itself. The world says, "Dum spiro, spero." The Christian can say, "Dum expiro, spero."

The Christian's Starting Place

"Ye are complete in him."—*Col. ii*, 10.

Do not make a goal of that which God makes a starting point lest you upset everything.

A Heavenly Magnet

"Set your affections on things above."—*Col. iii*, 2.

What beneath? Earth, principalities and powers. What above? Heaven and a Father's love.

Life—One Unbroken Thanksgiving

"Giving thanks to God and the Father by him."—*Col. iii*, 17.

Aim at perpetual union and making life one unbroken thanksgiving.

Grace to Preach

"Unto me, who am less than the least of all saints, is this grace given, that I should preach among the Gentiles the unsearchable riches of Christ."—*Eph. iii*, 8.

Keep me faithful, dear Lord, to the gift of grace and calling to the ministry. . . . Higher in Christ, lower in self. Blessed gift, grace to preach . . . of Christ.

Shamed

"And the priests and the Levites were ashamed, and sanctified themselves."—2 *Chron. xxx*, 15.

Let us rejoice even if shame be the sheep-dog to drive the shepherds.

Deliverance from Prison

"Bring my soul out of prison that I may praise thy name."
—*Ps. cxlii*, 7.

When filled with the Holy Spirit the spring is within, and rivers flow—no longer hard labour.

An Easy Yoke

"Take my yoke upon you, and learn of me."—*Matt. xi*, 29.

The soul's yoke. We must walk step by step with Him

to find it comfortable and easy. He gives rest and then we find it.

Singing and Praising

Unless we can sing with our lives, "Jesus is worthy to receive . . ." down here, how can we sing above?

"Go up from year to year to worship the King."
—*Zech. xiv*, 16.

Withhold praises and God will withhold blessings.

The Secret of Restoration

"If thou return to the Almighty."—*Job xxii*, 23.

If you have lost some of the peace once known, return. The shepherd's work is to take care of the sheep, not the sheep's to look after the shepherd, or a child to take care of the parent.

Divine Support Under Misunderstandings

It is a comparatively easy thing to bear misunderstanding from outsiders, but not so easy when the brethren misunderstand. At such times only the Divine Communion sustains the servant.

CHAPTER II

CHRISTIANS all the world over have for many years eagerly awaited the gracious utterances of Bishop Taylor Smith on all matters relating to consecration and holy living. A selection of his comments on passages in the Old and New Testaments, which are pointed in their suggestiveness, are given below. On the passage, "He is able even to subdue all things unto himself" (Phil. iii, 21) there is a beautiful personal note as follows: "Fulfil it to me, dear Lord, that I may be wholly thine." Many of the short paragraphs are heart-searching, but they are couched in terms that are winsome and likely to create desires for a closer walk with God.

The Day of Consecration

Shall we not mark the place where the Lord makes our path glorious? The day of consecration is the day of power and honour.

Yield Yourselves unto God

"And Jonathan climbed up upon his hands and upon his feet."—1 *Sam. xiv*, 13.

We know not by which member we shall bring glory to God and salvation to the people.

Seeing God

"I have heard of thee by the hearing of the ear, but now mine eye seeth thee."—*Job xlii*, 5.

Seeing is an advance on hearing. The secret of the changed life is seeing God—Moses, Joshua, Isaiah, Daniel, Philip, Paul, John.

White Garments

"Let thy garments be always white."—*Eccles. ix*, 8.

Such as make use of the blood of Christ, and daily try to keep garments white, shall receive white garments hereafter. Who walk in white robes of holiness here shall walk in white robes of glory hereafter. There are various degrees of sonship. Those who love closest will live closest.

Confide to Abide

"If ye will not believe, surely ye shall not be established."
—*Isa. vii*, 9.

If ye will not confide, ye shall not abide.

A Progressive Walk

"They . . . went backward and not forward."—*Jer. vii*, 24.

Looking at the map we note this. As pilgrims we ought to walk—progress. This must come from within, or is of no use. Christ was all for God. If we withhold ourselves we rob. Abraham walked the length and breadth of the promised land and claimed it.

Four Christian Qualities

"As for the likeness of their faces, they four had the face of a man, and the face of a lion, on the right side; and they four had the face of an ox on the left side: they four also had the face of an eagle."—*Ezek. i,* 10.

As Christians such must be our characteristics: 1. We must have the *sympathy* of a man—of Him who was called "Son of man" and His love for our fellows. 2. We must have the *boldness* of the lion—the Lion of the Tribe of Judah. 3. We must have the *patience, forbearance* and *suffering* of the ox. 4. We must be like the eagle, *ever soaring Heavenwards,* aspiring higher and ever coming nearer the Sun of Righteousness.

What is Denying Self?

"If any man will come after me, let him deny himself, and take up his cross daily and follow me."—*Luke ix,* 23.

To deny is to ignore one's self: the real displacement of self from the throne of life in its purpose and hopes, and the real enthronement of Another.

Followers who Follow

"And he led them out as far as to Bethany, and he lifted up his hands and blessed them."—*Luke xxiv,* 50.

He comes with angel carols, and departs with priestly benediction. Blessing is always to followers who follow near and hear His voice.

An Open Heaven

"Lo, the heavens were opened unto him."—*Matt. iii.* 16.

When we truly die unto sin then the Heavens are open.

Salvation and Sanctification

"And looking upon Jesus as he walked, he saith, Behold the Lamb of God."—*John i,* 36.

It is one thing to see Jesus coming to us—this is salvation, another to look upon Him as He walked and follow—this is sanctification.

Rill or Rivers?

"Rivers of living water."—*John vii,* 38.

Rivers depend on mountain tops, eh? Is there only a rill from you? It should be a river or rivers.

Two Distinguishing Marks

"My sheep hear my voice, and I know them, and they follow me."—*John x,* 27.

Christ's sheep have two marks—the ear and the foot—they hear and follow.

Clear Guidance

"And after he had seen the vision, immediately we endeavoured to go into Macedonia."—*Acts xvi,* 10.

Perfectly clear is our way when walking closely with Jesus.

Pilgrims on the Tramp

"They were strangers and pilgrims on the earth."
Heb. xi, 13.

Keep us on the tramp. May we not settle down till we reach the City.

Talents—a Loan

"And unto one he gave five talents, and to another two, and to another one. . . ."—*Matt. xxv*, 15.

Talents: Gifts, influence, money, knowledge, health, strength, time, senses, reason, memory, affections—all from God, a loan.

Convincing Testimony

"We have heard him ourselves and know that this is indeed the Christ the Saviour of the world."—*John iv*, 42.

Personal dealings with Christ soon convince.

Seasoned Speech

"Let your speech be always with grace seasoned with salt."
—*Col. iv*, 6.

It was said of Robert Hall, "He was witty, but his sallies never cost a saint a sigh, or a virgin a blush."

If Grace—then Holiness

"And he said unto me, My grace is sufficient for thee."
—*2 Cor. xii*, 9.

Is it? Then what answer does my life give as regards holiness?

A Devotional Prayer

Paul's prayer in Eph. i, 17-19. Grand prayer before reading God's word. Do live the Resurrection life in the Holy Ghost.

A Practical Application

"He is able to even subdue all things unto Himself."—*Phil. iii*, 21.

Oh, blessed truth. Fulfil it to me, dear Lord, that I may be wholly Thine.

A Meet Vessel!

"If a man therefore purge himself from these, he shall be a vessel unto honour, sanctified, and meet for the Master's use, and prepared unto every good work."—2 *Tim. ii*, 21.

To be a vessel meet for Christ's use, note what things must be shunned, and what sought. The more we follow that which is good, the faster and the further we shall flee from that which is evil, in imagination or thought (pictures), in word (spoken or read); in deed (actions follow thoughts and words).

Handicaps

"Let us lay aside every weight and the sin which doth so easily beset us."—*Heb. xii*, 1.

Old associations, customs, prejudices! Not one, but every sin, for to cherish any weight or sin is to handicap ourselves in the Heavenly race.

CHAPTER III

READING between the lines it may be seen how great a part prayer played in the Bishop's life and work. There are indications that, behind the public ministry there must have been much time and thought constantly given to prayer.

The pregnant observation written by the Bishop by the side of the words, "but we will give ourselves continually to prayer and to the ministry of the Word," viz. "Prayer, one half: first half: best half," is a very significant indication of what lay behind his gracious, rich and influential ministry, flowing out of a life in habitual nearness to God.

Qualifications for Intercessors

Who intercedes for his fellow men must not only live near, but draw near.

"And he said, Oh let not the Lord be angry, and I will speak yet but this once. Peradventure ten shall be found there."—*Gen. xviii*, 32.

Why did Abraham not ask on? God stopped when he stopped.

Prayers and praises go in pairs,
He hath praises who hath prayers.

When God answers prayer, let us go on and enrich those He brings to us.

Divine Wrestling

"And Jacob was left alone; and there wrestled a man with him till the breaking of the day."—*Gen. xxxii*, 24.

God wrestles with us in the dawning of the day of life.

The Power of Prayer

"And it came to pass when Moses held up his hand that Israel prevailed: and when he let down his hand, Amalek prevailed."—*Exod. xvii*, 11.

Prayer is not so much words as an attitude. The edge of Moses' prayer is sharper than young Joshua's sword.

Partnership

"As his part is that goeth down to the battle, so shall his part be that tarrieth by the stuff: they shall part alike." —*1 Sam. xxx*, 24.

Both the one who prays and the one who fights shall share the glory.

An Enheartening Type

"And king Solomon gave unto the queen of Sheba all her desire."—*1 Kings x*, 13.

What a type of what Christ gives us when we visit Him in prayer.

A Man of God's Prayer

"Then said Elijah unto the people, I, even I only, remain a prophet of the Lord; but Baal's prophets are four hundred and fifty men."—*1 Kings xviii*, 22.

One prayer from a man of God is better than four hundred

and fifty prayers from worldly men. What prayers ! Four
hundred and fifty priests but no answer. When the priests'
voices fail, ritual is resorted to. O what zeal ! ! What
devotion ! !

Prayer's Wide Range

"Son of man, I have made thee a watchman unto the
house of Israel."—*Ezek. iii*, 17.

An important position. The safety of a city may depend
on us. Let us give no uncertain cry.

The Sin of Ceasing to Pray

"He (Daniel) kneeled upon his knees three times a day
and prayed, and gave thanks before his God, as he did
aforetime."—*Dan. vi*, 10.

To cease to pray is to rob God of tribute and ourselves of
comfort. It is a good thing to have fixed hours for prayer
even if very busy.

The Most Important Work

"The harvest truly is great, but the labourers are few:
pray ye therefore the Lord of the harvest that he would send
forth labourers into his harvest."—*Luke x*, 2.

The first and most important work is to pray.

God's Kingdom First

"T.y kingdom come."—*Luke xi*, 2.

Before one prayer is allowed for self, foreign missions are
to be remembered.

A Wonderful Prayer

"If ye then, being evil, know how to give good gifts unto your children: how much more shall your heavenly Father give the Holy Spirit to them that ask him?"—*Luke xi*, 13.

The only prayer for sinners out of Christ. The Holy Spirit for all who ask, not only Christians, but sinners. A father is bound to supply his children with bread.

Houses of Prayer

"My house is the house of prayer."—*Luke xix*, 46.

When our hearts are not Houses of Prayer, then we are robbing God of glory and our fellow men of blessing.

A Very Wide Promise

"If ye abide in me, and my words abide in you, ye shall ask what ye will, and it shall be done unto you."—*John xv*, 7.

This promise is very wide; nothing is too small and nothing is too great to ask.

Continuance and its Reward

"These all continued with one accord in prayer and supplication."—*Acts i*, 14.

The secret of a good work.

Prayer in Proportion

"But we will give ourselves continually to prayer, and to the ministry of the word."—*Acts vi*, 4.

Prayer one half, first half, best half.

A Shower after Forgetfulness

"Then remembered I the word of the Lord."—*Acts xi*, 16.

Oft we forget our prayers and Christ's promises, until we have a shower, when we immediately look up.

The Demands of Prayer

"Continue in prayer and watch in the same with thanksgiving."—*Col. iv*, 2.

Prayer is a work demanding thought, care and preparation. Words without thought never to Heaven go.

A Key to God's Treasury

"I exhort therefore, that, first of all, supplications, prayers, intercessions, and giving of thanks, be made for all men."—
1 *Tim. ii*, 1.

Prayer gives a holy boldness and humble familiarity with God to all who use it. It is like a key whereby we may open God's treasury and take out plentiful mercy for ourselves and others.

Prayer on Behalf of Converts

"Without ceasing I have remembrance of thee in my prayers night and day."—2 *Tim. i*, 3.

May I pray like this for my converts and sons in the Lord Jesus.

CHAPTER IV

HUMILITY

FEW and fitting are the words written in the Bishop's private Bible about this attractive grace. But the words which are recorded reflect a sincere mind in which the grace of God so prevailed, that, unaffectedly and with naturalness, the writer urges that, when promoted, men should not forget to take a towel. A beautiful illustration of this is the story the Bishop frequently told of a visit to a park in York on a very hot day when he sat down, tired, beside a poor fellow, down and out. "I have never," he said, "seen a more dilapidated fellow since the days of my curacy." There he sat talking with him about the mystery of life and the mystery of suffering. Another man on the seat began to get restless and left. Soon his place was taken by a very well-dressed man, to whom the Bishop turned and said, "My friend here is suffering from heart disease. We have been talking about the mystery of pain. Are you a Christian?"

"Blessed title ' servant.' Not other do I crave." Again, the language befitting humility is used. Pupils in the School of Heavenly grace will gladly take this low place to qualify for spiritual honours.

Humility's Title

"Hast thou considered my *servant* Job?"—*Job i*, 8.

Blessed title "servant." Not other do I crave.

Humility's Likeness

" Depart from me; for I am a sinful man, O Lord."
—Luke v, 8.

The tree bearing most fruit comes nearest to the ground; the vessel with the heaviest cargo sinks deepest in water; so great blessings cause great humility.

" He that humbleth himself shall be exalted."—*Luke xiv,* 11.

" Humble we must be if to Heaven we go,
High is the roof there, but the door is low."

Humility's Brokenness

" God be merciful to me a sinner."—*Luke xviii,* 13.

When the spirit feels most, it can say least. There is one sentence of the publican to many of the Pharisee.

Humility's Utterance

" I am the voice of one crying in the wilderness."
—John i, 23.

Wonderful humility, a voice heard but not seen.

Humility's Pattern

Christ washing the disciples' feet.

What marvellous condescension and humility. What are we, dear Lord ? We could not look up to Thee, hadst Thou not first looked down. Such a conviction (that He was come from God) will make us willing to do anything for man. When promoted do not let us forget to take a towel.

Humility's Lessons

. . . Why look Ye so earnestly on us . . .

" The God of Abraham . . . hath glorified his Son Jesus."
—Acts iii, 13.

Peter had learned to drop "I" and point to a greater, viz.
Christ.   Useful men must be humbler.

Humility's Opportunity

"But God hath chosen the foolish things."—1 *Cor. i*, 27.

O God, what an opportunity thou hast here in Thy servant.

CHAPTER V

SERVICE

THE garnered stores of experience, ranging over nearly half a century of a unique life, are detailed in this treasury of the Bishop's Bible. There is a body of teaching of inestimable value for all who desire to work effectively for God. It is enhanced by the ripe experience of a long career, devoted to the service of God. The kind of equipment which is the *sine qua non* of successful service is so set forth that the best things are placed within the reach of all. How practical and searching are the Bishop's words on this topic. In one form or another, fellowship with God is stressed with vigour. "To work *for God outside*, we must be *with God inside*."

The simplest, the youngest, or the weakest Christian will find here encouraging words. So will the most experienced Christian. Nothing of importance in service seems overlooked. Are there difficulties? God ever assists. Are there promises? They must be claimed. Are there self-made plans? God sinks our ships if this is for our good. Do we need spiritual capital for the enterprise? The Lord supplies it. Do we cry out for God to work? He will do much if we let Him. Is there a stoppage in the wells of comfort? Dig them out again. Do we see only our small and meagre resources? We have a great God to trust in. Do we find nature prevails? It must die, that grace may live. Are we downhearted? A fourfold summons rings in our ears: "Be strong." Does man fail us? God gives more than His word. Are we lonely? God chooses a friend. Do we leave home and country for the Lord's sake? Then we get the reward. Do we need helpers? We may pray for such. Do we seek guidance? The Word of God provides it. What are the demands of service? "We must come down to touch, sigh with sympathy, look to Christ and then speak the word of power."

The whole of the teaching under this head seems to be summed up in the words, "Prove God's presence at every step."

God's Dwelling Place

The Church is still God's dwelling-place and His presence makes it dangerous to approach with unholy feet or hands.

A Worshipping Servant

"And it came to pass that when Abraham's servant heard their words, he worshipped the Lord. . . ."—*Gen. xxiv*, 52.

The servant seems to worship at every step.

Unstop the Wells

"The Philistines had stopped them (the wells) and filled them with earth."—*Gen. xxvi*, 15.

Has the world filled up any of your wells of comfort such as prayer, Bible reading, Divine service? If so,

dig them out again until they seek peace (see verse 28).
How the enemy strives as we dig the wells of living water.

To Learn of we must be With

"Thus shalt thou say unto the children of Israel, I AM
hath sent me unto you."—*Exod. iii*, 14.

"I Am" secures all for "My people" for ever.

To work for God *outside*, we must be with God *inside*
—the secret of His presence.

What a Great God can Use

Exodus IV. Surely the Bush is enough ! No. Then
more grace abounds. Who is a God like unto our God ?
It is not great means but a great God we need to trust in.
He can use a rod, a ram's horn, a barley cake, a sling, a
stone, a gourd, or a worm.

"If God be with me"

"And Moses said unto God, Who am I ?"—*Exod. iii*, 11.

It matters not who, or what I am, if God be with me.
God will manifest His power to His servants. No ordinary
education will suffice for God's service. Nature must die
that grace may live.

God Equips

"And Moses said before the Lord, Behold, I am of uncir-
cumcised lips, and how shall Pharaoh hearken unto me ?"—
Exod. vi, 30.

Whom God sends He equips. Why do men not trust?

The only Anxious Care Permitted

"The Lord your God hath given you rest, and hath given you this land. . . . Until the Lord have given your brethren rest."—*Joshua i*, 13, 15.

We must help them to overcome. We must not rest until our brethren are saved—this the only anxious care God permits—the care of souls. The rest will be more welcome after the fight.

A Repeated Call

Joshua I. When He calls His soldiers four times in one chapter to "be strong" He means it, and the strength is His own gift. Those best can command who know how to serve.

Scarlet Thread

"Behold, when we come into the land, thou shalt bind this line of scarlet thread in the window. . . ."—*Joshua ii*, 18.

What we serve and honour God with, He will bless and make useful to us.

Man's Word and God's

". . . Ye know in all your hearts and in all your souls that not one thing hath failed of all the good things which the Lord your God spake concerning you. . . ."—*Joshua xxiii*, 14.

Man often comes short of his word. God is ever giving more than His word.

True Service

"Let them that love him be as the sun when he goeth forth in his might."—*Judges v*, 31.

Love is the secret of all true service.

God chooses the Humble

"My family is poor in Manasseh, and I am the least of my father's house."—*Judges vi*, 15.

Humble ones are ever the chosen of God for service. Gideon's work had to begin at home. He was evidently a timid man (see the words, by night). God gives us confidence before leading us to victory. When we are in earnest, those we fear most are found on our side.

The Gift of a Companion

"But if thou fear to go down, go thou with Phurah, thy servant to the host."—*Judges vii*, 10.

How helpful a God-chosen friend to accompany us in our work for Him.

Typical

"And the three companies blew the trumpets, and brake the pitchers, and held the lamps in their left hands, and the trumpets in their right hands to blow withal: and they cried, The sword of the Lord, and of Gideon."—*Judges vii*, 20.

Typical of our victories by preaching the everlasting Gospel and holding forth the light given. (See 2 Cor. iv, 6, 7.)

The World's Lullaby

Whilst we allow ourselves to be lulled to sleep by the world, our spiritual strength is taken from us. Samson needed a lad to assist him to serve the Lord.

A Profitable Posture

"Sit still, my daughter, until thou know how the matter will fall."—*Ruth iii*, 18.

How much we learn when we take this position.

A Full Reward

"So Boaz took Ruth, and she was his wife."
—*Ruth iv*, 13.

Who leave home and country for Israel's God, never fail to receive the hundredfold, the full reward in this life present.

An Encouraging Sequence

". . . But stand thou still awhile, that I may show thee the word of God. Then Samuel took a vial of oil . . ."— 1 *Sam. ix*, 27, and *x*, 1.

The word of the Lord by His servants is ever followed by signs. Full directions: then Go, and lo ! I am with you manifestly.

Qualified Helpers

"A band of men whose hearts God had touched."
—1 *Sam. x*, 26.

Give me such to help, O Lord.

The Work of Two Men

"So the Lord saved Israel that day."—1 *Sam. xiv*, 23.

By two men—laymen—upon whom no holy oil had fallen.

Plain Direction

"I will show thee what thou shalt do."—1 *Sam. xvi*, 3.

God's will is ever made plain to all such as seek it.

Humble Service

"Behold, he keepeth the sheep."—1 *Sam. xvi*, 11.

God calls us to be His servants when we are doing our plain duty.

Our Father wants neither position, nor possession, but submission.

Thy Brethren

"Look how thy brethren fare."—1 *Sam. xvii*, 18.

As we do this are we used and blessed of God.

A Substitute Found

"And David rose up early in the morning and left the sheep with a keeper."—1 *Sam. xvii*, 20.

Let us ever provide a substitute when entering upon other work. A shepherd good and true !

The Importance of Motive

The testing point of service is not success, nor quantity, but motive. (See Mark ix, 41.)

John the Baptist was (1) an affectionate preacher, beseeching and pressing home the truth (2) a practical preacher quickening to duty (3) a popular preacher addressing the people according to their capacity, (4) an evangelical preacher directing them to Christ (5) a copious preacher declaring the whole counsel of God. He feared not kings fearing God. In the " many other things " of his exhortation no doubt they were equally good and faithful.

Worldly Wisdom—Penalties

"She (Michal) despised him in her heart."—2 *Sam. vi*, 16.

The worldly despise enthusiasm and go childless in consequence.

Difficulties—but God

"By my God have I leaped over a wall."—2 *Sam. xxii*, 30.

God ever assists His children over difficulties. Probably this refers to David's escapes; perhaps from Saul. We must do our best though, and our hindrances shall be our greatest helps, like steps added to our Heavenward ladder.

Happy and Happier

"Happy are thy men, happy are these thy servants which stand continually before thee and that hear thy wisdom."— 1 *Kings x*, 8.

How much happier those servants of God who in His House are ever praising Him.

The Ministry of a Widow

"Behold, I have commanded a widow woman there to sustain thee."—1 *Kings xvii*, 9.

God never closes one door without opening another.

God Sinks our Ships

"Jehoshaphat made ships of Tharshish to go to Ophir for gold: but they went not; for the ships were broken at Ezion-geber."—1 *Kings xxii*, 48.

How often the Lord disposes of our plans, all for our good ! He sinks our ships.

Walking with God

"And Elijah took his mantle and wrapped it together and smote the waters, and they were divided hither and thither so that they two went over on dry ground."—2 *Kings ii*, 8.

Prove God's presence at every step.

Man's Part—God's Part

"Thus saith the Lord, Make this valley full of ditches."
2 *Kings iii*, 16.

Faith and works go together. Do your duty and the Lord will fill the ditches.

Sure Guidance

"According to the law of thy God which is in thine hand."
—*Ezra vii*, 14.

In all work if there is not a text, there is a principle to

guide us in God's Word. May our hand cleave to the sword, and may we have Holy Ghost power to wield it.

Excavated Ears

"Mine ears hast thou opened."—*Ps. xl*, 6.

A servant needs ears to do as bid—hence excavated= making an ear not existing before.

Promise for Missionaries

"I the Lord have called thee in righteousness, and will hold thine hand, and will keep thee, and give thee for a covenant of the people, for a light of the Gentiles."—*Isa. xlii*, 6.

Splendid promise for a missionary. Promises, precious and plentiful, but we must give the hand to get.

Faithfulness Required

"But the house of Israel will not hearken unto thee; for they will not hearken unto me."—*Ezek. iii*, 7.

We have nothing to do with results. God only requires faithfulness.

Life at its Highest

"Seek ye me, and ye shall live."—*Amos v*, 4.

To seek God hourly is to live.

Cleansed and Clothed

"Behold, I have caused thine iniquity to pass from thee, and I will clothe thee with change of raiment."—*Zech. iii*, 4.

The purpose of our cleansing and clothing is that we may serve before God for ever.

The Secret Life

"Therefore, when thou doest thine alms, do not sound a trumpet before thee."—*Matt. vi*, 2.

The life of faith is distinctly an inward life; seen without only in proportion to its existence within.

Divine Capital

"Lord, thou deliveredst unto me five talents."—*Matt. xxv*, 20.

Christian worker, let us ever work with our Lord's capital, not our own.

Preaching by Word, Look and Deed

"And he ordained twelve, that they should be with him, and that he might send them forth to preach."—*Mark iii*, 14.

The purpose of every Divine call is to send us forth to preach by word, look and deed—to heal sin-sick souls and tell of victory over sin and Satan.

The Mainspring of Service

"Suffer little children to come unto me."—Luke xviii, 16.

Love to Christ is the qualification for shepherding the flock.

Love Remains

"Follow after love."—1 *Cor. xiv*, 1.

The scaffolding is indispensably necessary, but when the edifice is complete, it is taken down as an encumbrance. Love remains.

Changed Conditions

"When I sent you without purse and scrip and shoes, lacked ye anything? And they said, Nothing."—*Luke xxii*, 35.

The disciples of Jesus first went forth trusting in Providence, and lacked nothing, but when they went forth afterwards they had to use the ordinary means which men use in spreading the Gospel (no longer miraculous powers with them). Their work in the first place could only be done by particular men, but now it is otherwise. The Church (individual) is responsible with God now. All can (must) help. Go ye forth who love the Lord. Matt. xxviii, 19.

An Arresting Type

The feeding of the five thousand. Our sermons, lessons, are like these few loaves and fishes; but with Jesus behind them the thousands shall be fed. To use what we have is to get more—like the widow's cruse, the more drawn on the more given. The Divinity of Christ is seen in feeding five thousand, the humanity of Christ in giving thanks as a dependent creature.

1. Reckon up the means at our disposal.

2. Commit the same to Christ for blessing and increase.

3. Christ places the extension of His Kingdom in the hands of His servants.

The Demands of Service

"He touched his tongue; and looking up to heaven, he sighed."—*Mark vii* 33, 34.

Like Christ, we too must come down to touch, sigh with sympathy, look to Christ and then speak the word of power.

The Independence of God's Messengers

"I am Gabriel, that stand in the presence of God; and am sent to speak unto thee."—*Luke i*, 19.

When a man views himself as the messenger of God, he is quite at ease as to the reception of the message.

Before His Face

"Whither he himself would come."—*Luke x*, i.

Christ here sends His disciples only where He would go Himself. May we do so, going only where He is.

If we let God Work

"Follow thou me."—*John xxi*, 22.

The last command to Peter is the same as the first command to him (Matt. iv, 19).

How much God could and would do if we truly let Him.

Not Disobedient to the Heavenly Vision

"The Holy Spirit said, Separate me Barnabas and Saul."
—*Acts xiii.* 2.

God calls us when doing our present duty faithfully. To have stayed would have brought a curse and spiritual dry rot.

At one with God

"But this thou hast, that thou hatest the deeds of the Nicolaitans, which I also hate."—*Rev. ii*, 6.

Indifference to error may be deemed charity, but it is not so. God is jealous over us; we ought to be jealous for His glory.

CHAPTER VI

TESTIMONY

ALL Christians are called to bear testimony. By the fact of relationship with God, they are to show forth the praises of Him who called them out of darkness into His marvellous light. Life as well as lips ought to bear unceasing witness to the power of God's grace. There will be found in this chapter the assurance that although a Christian may be conscious of defect and deficiency, he may receive supplies to meet his need from Divine sufficiency. Wise teaching is given concerning witnessing in these words: "Refuse to argue and confess His power." The apparatus may be slender, but the sinner saved by grace "may be a blessing to the City." Consistency in living is vital for any effective testimony. The all-important qualification for all witnesses—the speaker and the non-speaker alike, is cogently summed up by the Bishop in these terms;—" Both need God with their mouth."

There is a valuable note against the words "And when they had prayed." Here it is: "The answer of their prayer was not manifested *until they tried to speak.*" Many a Christian worker fails at this point, expecting grace to be given beforehand. Grace is always given at the right moment, and faith rests in God expecting the supply to be given "in time of need."

Rewards for Sowing

"The thing proceedeth from the Lord."—*Gen. xxiv*, 50.

Such testimony environs the world.

Whenever we sow for the Lord we receive a reward in this world and in the next.

Moses said. The Lord said

"And Moses said unto the Lord, O, my Lord, I am not eloquent. . . . And the Lord said unto him, Who hath made man's mouth?"—*Exod. iv*, 10, 11.

Moses said, "I am not." God said, "I AM." Praise the Lord for this blessed reminder. The speaker Aaron and the non-speaker Moses both needed God with their mouths. Two are better than one, whether in labour, rest or conflict. Moses got only half the blessing God had in store for him. When God calls, how beautifully he prepares the man.

Sunshine after Rain

"And he shall be as the light of the morning, when the sun riseth, even a morning without clouds; as the tender grass springing out of the earth by clear shining after rain."—2 *Sam. xxiii*, 4.

A sunny day, increasing light with no earthborn clouds. Tender grass (young Christians, eh?) springing by our shining, after we have had the rain of trouble.

Dumbness Cured

"And he was casting out a devil, and it was dumb."
—*Luke xi*, 14.

May our dumb devils be all cast out. O Lord, open Thou my lips.

Full of Light

"If thy whole body therefore be full of light, having no part dark, the whole shall be full of light."—*Luke xi*, 36.

If the soul be not darkened with prejudice it shall be made fully light by the Holy Spirit.

Effective Personal Evangelism

"There was a man sent from God, whose name was John. The same came for a witness."—*John i*, 6, 7.

We may not all be able to argue, we can all witness, however. Refuse to argue and confess His power.

"And the two disciples heard him speak, and they followed Jesus."—*John i*, 37.

The fruits of faithful testimony,—exalting Christ, not the church, or anything else. Knowing the Saviour ourselves ought to make us evangelists to others.

An Encouraging Example

"Come, see a man, which told me all things that ever I did: is not this the Christ?"—*John iv*, 29.

An open-air preacher without college training, who took her hearers to Jesus, and they were saved. A sinner by grace made a blessing to the city. Christians work on.

Hidden

"He expounded unto them in all the scriptures the things concerning himself."—*Luke xxiv*, 27.

As our Lord did, so ought we, to hide behind the Scriptures that ourselves may not be seen.

Many Other Things

"And there are also many other things which Jesus did. . . ."
—*John xxi*, 25.

Like John, we can't tell all we know.

Grace Given at the Right Moment

"And when they had prayed."—*Acts iv*, 31.

The answer of their prayer was not manifested until they tried to speak.

The Power of Influence

". . . That at the least the shadow of Peter passing by might overshadow some of them."—*Acts v*, 15.

Influence is like a shadow, the greater where the light is brightest. A holy man influences he knows not whom.

We can but tell the works, the Holy Spirit alone can give life.

The Church's Witness

"To the intent that now unto the principalities and powers in heavenly places might be known by the church the manifold wisdom of God."—*Eph. iii*, 10.

God's people are like the child in the midst, set to teach angels in Heaven.

Paul's Wonderful Life

"For to me to live is Christ."—*Phil. i*, 21.

Here is the secret of the wonderful life of St. Paul.

Truth through Personality—Its Atmosphere

"Speaking the truth in love."—*Eph. iv,* 15.

Truth is to become incarnate, personal, in us. We must hold fast to it, speak it, live it. Truth is to be the centre and vital force, love the atmosphere and environment.

The Sin of Inconsistency

"Only let your conversation be as it becometh the gospel of Christ."—*Phil. i,* 27.

The discrepancy between the creed of Christian men and their daily conduct is a terrible sin, and a tremendous curse.

A Personal Testimony

"The Lord knoweth how to deliver the godly out of temptations."—2 *Pet. ii,* 9.

Praise the Lord He does it !

CHAPTER VII

SOUL-WINNING

THE Bishop was pre-eminently a soul winner. The books in his library on the subject of this great enterprise are heavily marked, revealing his discriminating and keen observation. His sermons and public addresses abound in illustrations of fishing for men and catching them. He was the most attentive and appreciative listener to stories others had to tell of soul-winning and was a great encourager to all who sought the spiritual welfare of men. The recorded thoughts of the Bishop in his Bible constitute gems of rare value, and are of such a character as to instruct, encourage and stimulate efforts for continuous personal evangelism.

Six Important Matters

(1) If we are to catch men, we must go after them as fishers after fish.

(2) It is not enough to open nets, and wish them in.

(3) All fishing grounds are not of equal importance, some are better than others, as the square, the market-place, the mountain-side, the Temple court, Mars' Hill, Cæsar's palace—these are the fishing grounds of Apostles.

(4) Whilst close season in fishing—none in men fishing.

(5) Needful preparation. See that lines, hooks and nets are in order.

(6) Be sure there is a hook on every line, and remember, catching means pain.

An Encouraging Promise

"Fear not, thou shalt have this son also."—*Gen. xxxv*, 17. So often when trying to give birth to a sinner, we despair. God comforts us with this promise.

Many Sheaves

"And none shall appear before me empty."
—*Exod. xxxiv*, 20.

Having been redeemed, let none appear before God empty. May we have many sheaves to lay at His feet—souls and praises.

A Vital Contact Essential

"And he (Elisha) went up and lay upon the child, and put his mouth upon his mouth and his eyes upon his eyes, and his hands upon his hands; and he stretched himself upon the child, and the flesh of the child waxed warm."—*2 Kings iv*, 34.

We must lay our moral and spiritual nature over that of the person we wish to restore. There must also be the breath of the Divine life received through us.

A Holy Alliance

"The fruit of the righteous is a tree of life; and he that winneth souls is wise."—*Prov. xi*, 30.

What God hath joined together, let no man put asunder—holy living and soul-winning.

Immeasurable Possibilities

"And they that shall be of thee shall build the old waste places: thou shalt raise up the foundations of many generations."—*Isa. lviii*, 12.

Each soul converted is a foundation upon which others shall be built. Who can tell the crop from the seed of one soul?

Urgency Needed

"They sought means to bring him in, and to lay him before him."—*Luke v*, 18.

If souls are to be blessed, we must be pressing and urgent.

Not too Weary

"Jesus therefore, being weary with his journey, sat thus on the well."—*John iv*, 6.

Weary, but not too weary to save souls. Jesus forgets His own need in thinking of this poor woman's need.

It is Time to Reap

"Say not ye, There are yet four months and then cometh harvest? Behold, I say unto you, Lift up your eyes and look on the fields; for they are white already to harvest."
—*John iv*, 35.

Have we not sown enough? Surely it is time to reap. We say, "Four months," Jesus says, "Now ready." Our joy is full as we lead souls to Christ.

Fisherman and Shepherd

"He (Jesus) saith unto him, Feed my lambs."—*John xxi*, 15.

The fisher for souls must also turn shepherd. These last words are like mother's last words to children keeping house, "Take care of baby." Perhaps Peter had been one who sent children away, but now he is told to feed them. The most precious charge which cost Christ so much—the sheep and the lambs.

An Unceasing Mission

"But when he was in Rome he sought me out very diligently and found me."—2 *Tim. i*, 17.

A good man is ever seeking out people—worldly people for Christ: Christians for Christ.

As the Stars

"And they that turn many to righteousness as the stars for ever and ever."—*Dan. xii*, 3.

Degrees in heaven—talents used—crown won—each gem a ransomed soul to cast at Jesus' feet. Amen.

PART III

CHAPTER I

SIN

IT has been said that every heresy is rooted in defective views of sin. The quotations reproduced in this chapter show that the Bishop wrote strong words about sin. In his treatment of this awful evil, there are no illusions as to sin's destructive and devastating power, nor does he entertain any doubt whatsoever that its presence within the Christian remains whilst life lasts. The means by which sin may be counteracted is stated in plain words, viz. "*cast out and kept out.*" These are the crucial terms —indicating decision and conflict, "crisis and process." The whole handling of the subject is Scriptural and vigorous, and it will be welcomed for its wholesome instruction. It is calculated to stir faltering combatants to fresh courage in this conflict from which there is no discharge. Many a lengthy treatise which has for its aim a complete treatment of this theme lacks the point, pungency and effectiveness of these arresting and penetrating sentences from the Bishop's pen. It is indeed touching to see Bishop Taylor Smith's initials inscribed against the words: "Spare not the king of our besetting sin, but hew it in pieces before God. So let thine enemies in me perish, O Lord. J.T.S."

A Startling Alternative

"There is an accursed thing in the midst of thee, O Israel; thou canst not stand before thine enemies, until ye take away the accursed thing from among you."—*Joshua vii*, 13.

Either we must destroy it, or it will destroy us (any known wilful sin).

Spare It Not!

"And Samuel hewed Agag in pieces before the Lord in Gilgal."—1 *Sam. xv*, 33.

Spare not the king of our besetting sin, but hew it in pieces before God. So let Thine enemies perish in me O Lord. J.T.S. (J. Taylor Smith.)

A Little or Big Amalek

"Now go and smite Amalek and utterly destroy all that they have and spare them not." —1 *Sam. xv*, 3.

A plain command. Amalek is typical of sin. All to be utterly destroyed. The little Amalek will only grow into a big Amalek.

Grace the Only Security

"For it came to pass, when Solomon was old, that his wives turned away his heart after other gods."—1 *Kings xi*, 4.

Nothing forms in itself a security against the deceitfulness and depravity of the human heart. Nor will old age cure the heart of any propensity. God's grace alone can overcome sinful passions. We are pilgrims in an enemy's country, therefore need to watch and pray.

The Rebuke of the World

"But if ye say unto me, We trust in the Lord our God; is not that he whose high places and whose altars Hezekiah hath taken away."—2 *Kings xviii*, 22.

How powerful the rebuke when the world seizes hold of our inconsistencies and sins.

Besetting Sin—the Antidote

Having prayed against your besetting sin, do you work and watch?

The Nets of Sin

"Pull me out of the net that they have laid privily for me."—*Ps. xxxi*, 4.

How many and strong are the nets of sin.

Whiter than Snow

"Wash me, and I shall be whiter than snow."—*Ps. li*, 7.

Sin like leprosy may make us white as snow—only Christ can make us whiter.

How to Conquer an Old Habit

"He began to curse and to swear, saying, I know not this man of whom ye speak."—*Mark xiv*, 71.

Had Peter been watchful and prayerful his old sailor habit could not have returned.

Sin Cast Out and Kept Out

"And he went into the temple, and began to cast out them that sold therein and them that bought."—*Luke xix*, 45.

He cast out, but did not destroy—so with sin. Whilst Christ abides within, sin is cast out and kept out.

A Christian cannot Live in Sin

"For sin shall not have dominion over you."—*Rom. vi*, 14.

It is possible for a Christian to be drawn into any sin—impossible for him to remain in it.

The Progress of an Evil Word

"And the tongue is a fire, a world of iniquity."—*Jas. iii*, 6.

Master the tongue and you can master all else. The sin of the tongue is not the sin of a moment: it goes on. A beast is tamed, a fire burns out, but progress of an evil word cannot be stopped. On, on! A battlefield is disproportionate to a country lost or won on it—so with the tongue. The great Fire of London began in a little shop but destroyed from Tower to Temple.

CHAPTER II

THE MYSTERIES OF LIFE

THE experience of mankind in all ages confirms the fact that events happen in men's lives for which there often is no complete or satisfying explanation. The children of God are not exempt from mysterious accidents, losses, deprivations. Loss of health, loss of wealth, loss of business, loss by illness, loss by sudden death and in countless ways come alike to all. The prosperity of unscrupulous men, the temporary adversity of godly men, the apparent triumph of evil, the discords of life, the separations, the misunderstandings, the alienations, and a thousand other happenings—these afflict men everywhere. The Christian man has a refuge in God. He may speak out his grievance within the sanctuary, and therein find, where the balances swing true and free, that he may "understand," as Asaph did, some things that sorely pained him outside the sanctuary (See Ps. lxxiii). It is a good starting point when "sorrows like sea-billows roll" to affirm with Abraham (as the Bishop enjoins in the first quoted sentence): "Shall not the Judge of all the earth do right ?" Then again: "The darkness drew them nearer: so may we be led by the shadows of adversity." What a brave and uplifting thought, especially if the Christian man recognizes that God is over all.

"God moves in a mysterious way
His wonders to perform;
He plants His footsteps in the sea
And rides upon the storm.

Deep in unfathomable mines
Of never-failing skill,
He treasures up His bright designs
And works His sovereign Will.

Judge not the Lord by feeble sense,
But trust Him for His grace;
Behind a frowning providence
He hides a smiling face.

Blind unbelief is sure to err
And scan His work in vain;
God is His own Interpreter
And He will make it plain."

The Bishop's recorded thoughts about the doubts of
Thomas and how they turned to glorify God, and the practical exhortation to touch the Lord, by faith, will doubtless
come as a benediction, and bring spiritual healing to many.

An Example to be Imitated

We cannot understand God's dealings with us, yet
let us say with Abraham, Shall not the Judge of all the
earth do right ?

Eden and Gethsemane

"In the sweat of thy face shalt thou eat bread."
—*Gen. iii*, 19.

Christ removed this by sweat in Gethsemane.

" Sun, Stand Thou Still "

"He (Joshua) said in the sight of Israel, Sun, stand thou still upon Gibeon."—*Joshua x*, 12.

As this was a check on the approaching night, so it was when Christ came, the true Sun of righteousness, the Light of the world. There is no reason to think the earth stayed in her course, God could produce by reflection that appearance which gave continued light called by man the sun standing still—perhaps by vapour, most probably the earth was stopped by God, as one stops a watch by holding the balance.

A Purpose for Every Life

"Thus saith the Lord, thy redeemer, and he that formed thee from the womb."—*Isa. xliv*, 24.

He that formed me did so for a purpose.

An Important Distinction

"The soul that sinneth it shall die. The son shall not bear the iniquity of the father."—*Ezek. xviii*, 20.

The body of a son may suffer for his father's sin, not so the soul.

Mysterious Developments

"A certain nobleman went into a far country to receive for himself a kingdom and to return."—*Luke xix*, 12.

Christ went to receive a Kingdom, leaving two classes of people, servants and citizens.   When He returns He finds servants and rebels.

The Ministry of Adversity

"And all his acquaintance, and the women that followed him from Galilee, stood afar off, beholding these things."
—*Luke xxiii*, 49.

But the darkness drew them nearer: so may we be led by the shadows of adversity.

All Nature a Miracle

Christ turns the water into wine.   A miracle, true.   But is not all nature a miracle, a little less time used here, eh ?

A Marvellous Over-ruling

The very doubts of Thomas turned to glorify God and give us proof of the resurrection.

"Reach hither thy hand and thrust it into my side."
—*John xx*, 27.

Let us not fail to touch, and have all doubt removed.

Converting Daily Wants

Turn your daily wants into daily prayers, and God will turn your daily prayers into daily praises.

CHAPTER III

LITTLE THINGS

"Even a leaf, a flower, a worm, are God's stewards with measured power for allotted ends." If this is true in nature, what shall be said of man, renewed by the grace of God and brought into fellowship with God? Who would be so bold as to estimate either the importance or privilege of a Christian placing his life within the ordered government of God, and applying to his own life the words of Holy Scripture: "In *all* thy ways acknowledge Him and He shall direct thy paths"? As it is probably true that no man has the power to gauge the value or quality of what are called little things, it becomes imperative to refer all matters to God that the "government may be upon His shoulders." Life easily develops in directions away from God. If a road is taken which has an almost imperceptible curve, a traveller will find himself far from his purposed destination the further he goes on the road.

The Harvest of a Single Act

"In all thy ways acknowledge him, and He shall direct thy paths."—*Prov. iii, 6.*

How necessary to be kept seeing that our future depends or may be influenced by a single act.

Lambs

"He shall gather the lambs with his arms."—*Isa. xl*, 11.

Lambs first again.

Life's Composition

"A little one shall become a thousand and a small one a strong nation: I the Lord will hasten it in his time."
—*Isa. lx*, 22.

"Whosoever therefore shall break one of these least commandments, and shall teach men so he shall be called the least in the Kingdom of Heaven."—*Matt. v*, 19.

It is the little actions for good or evil which tell; character, life, everything is made up of little things.

Avoid—Mortify

"And if thy right eye offend thee, pluck it out."
—*Matt. v*, 29.

Avoid the first springs or occasions of evil desire, even by the sacrifice of what is most useful and dear to us. Many have been destroyed by neglecting to mortify one single member.

" All Things serve His Might "

"And there arose a great storm of wind. . . . And he was in the hinder part of the ship asleep on a pillow."
—*Mark iv*, 37, 38.

"Rocked in the cradle of the deep"—His Father's hand on the cradle. The winds, waves, and clouds are only God's servants. Even a leaf, a flower, a worm are God's stewards, with measured power for allotted ends. Talk of all His wondrous works to us. "Like as a father pitieth his children, so the Lord pitieth them that fear him."

Ananias Teaches Saul

An obscure believer (Ananias, Acts ix) does a mighty work, teaching Saul the greatest of New Testament blessings, viz. the filling of the Holy Spirit. We need to be filled for such work.

The Power of Little Things

"A little leaven leaveneth the whole lump."—1 *Cor. v*, 6.

A mist, a slip of the hand, or voice, has often turned a battle ! Behold the power of a spark.

Hinges of Gold

"And the hinges of gold."—1 *Kings vii*, 50.

Little things, yet great doors swung open by them. Out of sight, yet result seen. Gold—smooth, soft, gentle, no rust, no squeaking or discordant noise.

CHAPTER IV

In a world like this, and in an age of rush, tumult, restlessness and uncertainty, there is always a pavilion of rest and comfort whereto the child of God may continually resort. But for the trials and conflicts of life, for the sorrows and afflictions, he needs "words that sustain." (See Isa. 1, 4 R.V. marg.) Every true teacher of the word of God learns to comfort others by the comfort wherewith he himself has been comforted of God.

The quotations which form this chapter are full of comfort and consolation for tried saints. "Give me ever bitter waters for God to sweeten; then sweet waters to intoxicate and teach me to forget." The waters are bitter, but Divine alchemy changes their quality. Or consider the luxury of leaning on the Divine Arm "every day and all the day, to defend from danger and to keep from sin, to uphold under all circumstances, every burden, to lean on when weary in the journey. God says: 'Let him take hold of My strength.'"

The Scripture "Behold I am the Lord, the God of all flesh, is there anything too hard for me?" has comforted vast numbers of God's people in all ages. The Bishop's marginal note, answering the Scripture question is golden. "No, dear Lord. Therefore do Thine utmost *to* me and *through* me." Such abandonment to the will of God expressed in the two prepositions makes a highway in the heart for God to fulfil His purposes.

The description of the storm on the sea of Galilee is unforgettable. "He knows every billow. . . . Here is the big Lord and the little me. If we look at trial we shall be afraid, but if at Him who sends it we shall feel nothing can separate." Here is a summons to every storm-tossed soul to commit himself to God.

There are two very comforting words about the departed. The first is a comment on the words "He anointed the eyes of the blind man with clay." The Bishop's comment is: "This is prophetic of the burial of our dead to awaken in the light of Heaven's brightness." The other comforting word is "Jesus is the only man who ever died—ours will be but a sleep. The words mean what they say."

Thrones

God made a throne of Sinai's granite head, and will of thy poor stony heart, O sinner.

The Sun Behind Clouds

Clouds, like trials, do not stop the sun from shining.

What Changes

". . . In the habitation of dragons, where each lay, shall be grass with reeds and rushes."—*Isa. xxxv*, 7.

What changes by God's Holy Spirit! Instead of jackals, we shall have reeds for light and music.

Divine Transmutation

"And the Lord shewed him a tree which, when he had cast into the waters, the waters were made sweet."
—*Exod. xv,* 25.

Give me ever bitter waters for God to sweeten, then sweet waters to intoxicate and teach me to forget. (See Rom. v, 3-5.) Only in the wilderness can we gain our experience of God's love and power and get to know ourselves. Elim far exceeds Marah; there are more sweets than bitters even in wilderness experience.

Great Peace

"And all thy children shall be taught of the Lord, and great shall be the peace of thy children."—*Isa. liv,* 13.

Great teaching and great peace, eh?

Costly Gifts Gratis

"Ho, every one that thirsteth, come ye to the waters, and he that hath no money; come ye, buy, and eat; yea, come, buy wine and milk without money and without price."
—*Isa. lv,* 1.

No special thirst is here mentioned. Many thirst indefinitely, but God is the need. What cost God everything costs man nothing.

A Christian's Portion

"Then shall thy light rise in obscurity, and thy darkness be as the noonday. And the Lord shall guide thee continually and satisfy thy soul in drought."—*Isa. lviii,* 10, 11.

Even the darkest aspect of a true Christian should exceed the brightest aspect of the world. If the Lord guides and satisfies continually we cannot help bringing forth fruit continually and being made refreshing sources to all mankind.

An Exceeding Great and Precious Promise

"O Lord, be gracious unto us; we have waited for thee: be thou their arm every morning."—*Isa. xxxiii,* 2.

To lean upon *every day and all the day*, to defend from danger and to keep from sin, to uphold under all circumstances, every burden, to lean on when weary in the journey. God says, "Let him take hold of my strength."

Anything too Hard?

"Behold, I am the Lord, the God of all flesh, is there anything too hard for me?"—*Jer. xxxii,* 27.

No, dear Lord. Therefore do thine utmost *to* me and *through* me.

Nothing is adversity to the child of God.

A Mistaken Calculation

"Seek ye first the kingdom of God and his righteousness, and all these things shall be added unto you."—*Matt. vi, 33.*

Not taken away as some seem to think.

Tell Jesus

>   . . . "and went and told Jesus."—*Matt. xiv,* 12.

Here in Him alone, who never fails us, do we find sweet sympathy.

The big Lord and the little me in a Storm

> "Jesus went unto them, walking on the sea."
> —*Matt. xiv,* 25.

He knows every billow! Christ prays whilst we toil. He will come sooner or later to rescue, for the promise is "never leave, nor forsake." Here is the big Lord and the little me. If we look at trial we shall be afraid, but if at Him who sends it we shall feel nothing can separate. Those who are with Jesus in a storm shall profit by the storm.

A Living Saviour

The secret of a nation's peace is Christ recognized, the secret of domestic joy is Christ in the midst of home, the secret of the world's regeneration is Christ in the midst. The ship which carries a Jonah in it though strongly built will founder in a storm, but that ship containing a living Saviour will never suffer shipwreck but will reach the haven of peace.

And Peter!

> "But go your way, tell his disciples and Peter that he goeth before you into Galilee."—*Mark xvi.* 7.

And Peter, How sweet, eh?

Healing for the Broken-Hearted

"And she stood at his feet behind him weeping, and began to wash his feet with tears."—*Luke vii*, 38.

Her eyes had been the inlets and outlets of sin. Only the broken-hearted prove the preciousness of Jesus. The self-sufficient are disgusted at the love of sinners.

He Talked with Them

"And they said one to another, Did not our heart burn within us while he talked with us by the way ?—*Luke xxiv*, 32.

He will warm up any hearts He talks with.

A Great Contrast

"Two hundred pennyworth of bread is not sufficient for them that everyone of them may take a little."—*John vi*, 7.

Man speaks of "a little." Christ gives "as much as they would."

A Glorious Prospect

"He anointed the eyes of the blind man with the clay."
—*John ix*, 6.

This is prophetic of the burial of our dead, to awaken in the light of Heaven's brightness.

The Omnipresent Christ

"Jesus saith unto her, Woman, why weepest thou ? Whom seekest thou ?"—*John xx*, 15.

How often we fret and worry seeking Jesus, whilst all the time He is standing near.

Re-instated

"They went up into an upper room, where abode Peter
. . . and Thomas. . . ."—*Acts i*, 13.

Though Peter denied and Thomas doubted, yet they are
here, forgiven and reinstated.

The Cheer of Fellowship

"When the brethren heard of us, they came to meet us
as far as Appii forum. . . ."—*Acts xxviii*, 15.

How often God thus cheers us on our way, by sending the
brethren to us, eh?

He Died—We Sleep

"For if we believe that Jesus died and rose again, even
so them also which sleep in Jesus will God bring with Him."
—1 *Thess. iv*, 14.

Jesus is the only man who ever died—ours will be but a
sleep. The words mean what they say.

What to do with Cares

"Casting all your care upon him, for He careth for you."
—1 *Pet. v*, 7.

All the small cares with the large ones, small flies and pin
scratches hurt more than big ones, eh?

A Refined Estimate

"Grace be with you, mercy, and peace, from God the Father, and from the Lord Jesus Christ, the Son of the Father, in truth and love."—2 *John*, 3.

As John draws near the evening of life the two things dearest to his heart are ever on his lips—truth and love.

PART IV

CHAPTER I

THE records in this chapter show the Bishop as a graphic artist. The references make ancient scenes reappear in homely beauty, and Bible figures stand out in vivid portraiture. Through his pen, a sentence contains a sermon, and half a dozen words illuminate an old theme. The swift observation reveals more than the laboured discourse, and the few well-chosen words are pregnant with meaning. The terse phrase holds much truth. Here are seed thoughts for the mind, food for the imagination, and comfort for the heart. Through the ordinary and everyday occurrence and the familiar reference, truths shine as lustrous gems.

A Primitive, Patriarchal Scene

"Let a little water, I pray you, be fetched, and wash your feet and rest yourselves *under the tree*."—*Gen. xviii*, 4.

Primitive dining-room. Hearty friendship stoops to anything but sin. Christ washed feet.

"And Abraham hastened into the tent unto Sarah and said, Make ready quickly . . . and make cakes. . . . And Abraham ran."—*Gen. xviii*, 6, 7.

Sarah—handsome in action, as well as in looks—could cook ! Abraham a model husband, unselfish—and though one hundred years old, he ran. Butter, bread, milk and veal, by no means bad fare !

No Luggage Allowed!

"Escape for thy life: look not behind thee, neither stay thou in all the plain."—*Gen. xix*, 17.

No luggage allowed! So in leaving the world!

Old Aaron Ran

"And the servant ran to meet her."—*Gen. xxiv*, 17.

Few Simons nowadays. Running unbecoming, eh? Old Aaron ran, and plague stopped. Prodigal's father ran.

A Sinister Development

"And Esau hated Jacob . . . and Esau said in his heart."
—*Gen. xxvii*, 41.

No doubt this smothered hate developed into muttered threat.

The Inseparable Presence

"And Joseph was brought down to Egypt. . . . And the Lord was with Joseph."—*Gen. xxxix*, 1, 2.

Our enemies may rob us of much, but they cannot take from us wisdom and grace, or separate us from the presence of the Lord.

Noble

"And he (Joseph) comforted them and spake kindly to them."—*Gen. l*, 21.

Noble fellow!

Drilling Recruits

"Fear ye not, stand still and see the salvation of the Lord."—*Exod. xiv*, 13.

The first attitude of faith is to stand still. It is easier to go, to do, but recruits must be drilled ere efficiency is reached. Restlessness can neither add to our stature nor change the colour of our hair. Neither Israel, nor we, can scatter Egyptians, level the mountains or dry up the sea. Running people don't see things properly. Why bring a lighted candle to help the sun?

Transformed Mirrors !

"And he made the laver of brass and the foot of it of brass, of the looking-glasses of the women assembling. . . ."
—*Exod. xxxviii*, 8.

Probably to put a stop to their bringing of mirrors. (See 1 Pet. iii, 3, 4.)

The Peril of Self-will

"And God came unto Balaam at night, and said unto him, If the men come to call thee, rise up and go with them."
—*Num. xxii*, 20.

When we are determined to have our own way, God sometimes allows it, to our own hindrance.

Animals' Gifts

"And the ass saw the angel of the Lord standing in the way."—*Num. xxii*, 23.

Some animals have gifts men have not.

The One Fountain

"Hear, O Israel: The Lord our God is one Lord."
                                        —*Deut. vi*, 4.

One fountain better than 1,000 cisterns, eh? One all-sufficient God, than 1,000 inefficient friends.

A Selfish Provision

"What meaneth then this bleating of the sheep in mine ears, and the lowing of the oxen which I hear?"—1 *Sam. xv*, 14.

Selfish, for they no doubt expected a feast.

Appearances and Actuality

"But the Lord said unto Samuel, Look not on his countenance."—1 *Sam. xvi*, 7.

We can tell how people look; but only God can tell what they are.

Saul—King and Coward

"And Saul said to David, Thou art not able to go against this Philistine to fight with him."—1 *Sam. xvii*, 33.

How we judge others by ourselves. Saul was King and coward, tallest in height, shortest in courage!

David—Carrier and Conqueror

"And Jesse said unto David his son, Take now . . . these ten loaves . . . and carry these ten cheeses unto the captain of their thousand. . . ."—1 *Sam. xvii*, 17, 18.

The bread and cheese carrier made a mighty conqueror for God. " Out of the mouths of babes." . . . " God hath chosen." . . . (1 *Cor. i*, 27.)

An Ideal Wife

"Abigail; and she was a woman of good understanding, and of a beautiful countenance."—1 *Sam. xxv*, 3.

What more can a man wish for in a wife.

The Best Commendation

"And Micaiah said, As the Lord liveth, what the Lord saith unto me, that will I speak."—1 *Kings xxii*, 14.

Well done, Micaiah !

Bees

"They compassed me about like bees."—*Ps. cxviii*, 12.

Bees have stings as well as beings.

Time and Money Wasted

"In that day the Lord will take away the bravery of their tinkling ornaments about their feet, and their cauls, and their round tires like the moon, &c."—*Isa. iii*, 18.

The prophet must have had a peep into the ladies' wardrobes in Jerusalem. Disease follows pride. Tight lacing and boots: paint and powder, low dresses and colds, vinegar and whiteness, belladonna and enlarged pupils. Waste of time and money.

I

Praying Sisters.

"Mary and her sister Martha."—*John xi*, 1.

Happy the man with such sisters, praying ones, eh? Mary shines out most in Luke x, Martha in John xi.

Honest Toil

Christ was not ashamed of a workman's shop nor Paul of honest labour.

The First Theological College

"They (Aquila and Priscilla), . . . took him (Apollos) unto them and expounded unto him the way of God more perfectly."—*Acts xviii*, 26.

The first Theological Seminary was a humble lodging, a student, two professors, the woman the head.

Awkward Situations

"A certain man went down from Jerusalem to Jericho, and fell among thieves, which stripped him of his raiment, and wounded him, and departed, leaving him half dead."
—*Luke x*, 30.

It is bad enough to be in health without a pocket handkerchief—how much more, bleeding to death without a rag.

Herod the Fox

"The same day there came certain of the Pharisees, saying unto him, Get thee out and depart hence; for Herod will kill thee."—*Luke xiii*, 31.

Herod no doubt, afraid of Jesus, sent them. Foxy, eh?

Love Wins

"So they ran both together and the other disciple did outrun Peter."—*John xx*, 4.

Love ever outruns zeal.

Bad Manners and Christian Courtesy

"And about the time of forty years suffered he their manners in the wilderness."—*Acts xiii*, 18.

And they were bad manners ! Christian carefulness avoids giving offence or pain, and when given, tries to soothe.

An Approach through Parables

As in our Lord's time, so now, those whose minds are useless for want of exercise must be appealed to in an attractive form, viz., by parables. There are those able to judge the seasons, etc., but are ignorant of spiritual truths.

CHAPTER II

THE Bishop's wide sympathies and contact with all sorts and conditions of men are clearly reflected in the items of very varied scenes and places and people which are given in this section of the book. His amazing common-sense and vivid sketches need no commendation. The pithy comments, so characteristic of the Bishop, can be seen in almost every remark he records. Bible students will find not only hints and suggestions, but the element of joyful surprise and edification as they read this human document.

When God Trains

"Then answered one of the servants, and said, Behold, I have seen a son of Jesse the Beth-lehemite, that is cunning in playing, and a mighty valiant man, and a man of war, and prudent in matters, and a comely person, and the Lord is with him."—1 *Sam. xvi*, 18.

How beautifully God arranges for David to be taught court life. A servant is the instrument God often uses— Pharaoh's butler for Joseph; Naaman's maid. Domestics, you may be a blessing if Christians. God chooses the place of our abode.

Seize Opportunities

"And I said unto the king, If it please the king, and if

thy servant have found favour in thy sight, that thou wouldest
send me unto Judah, unto the city of my fathers' sepulchres,
that I may build it."—*Neh. ii, 5.*

Seize your opportunities for doing and getting good.

Labour !

"Man goeth forth unto his work and to his labour until
the evening."—*Ps. civ, 23.*

Labour whether we use pen or pickaxe.

Mind your own Business

"Lord, are there few that be saved ?"—*Luke xiii, 23.*

Never mind the few or the many, mind your own business.

A Wise Policy

"The Lord commended the unjust steward."—*Luke xvi, 8.*

The Lord commended not the fraud but the policy of his
servant.

The Subject of Conversation

"Again the next day after John stood, and two of his
disciples."—*John i, 35.*

Let us not be ashamed to point to Jesus in our conversation.

Hiding the Master

"But Mary stood without at the sepulchre weeping."
                                        —*John xx, 11.*

Earth-born tears and fears often obscure the Master.

Removing Grave Clothes

> "And he that was dead came forth, bound hand and foot
> with grave-clothes: and his face was bound about with a
> napkin. Jesus saith unto them, Loose him, and let him go."
> —*John xi*, 44.

Our duty is to clear away the grave-clothes from such
and their faces and mouths that we may show forth
Christ's praise.

Devotedness

> "Now there stood by the cross of Jesus his mother, and
> his mother's sister, Mary the wife of Cleophas, and Mary
> Magdalene."—*John xix*, 25.

To their eternal honour be it known; women stayed while
men fled.

A Soldier Praises

> "Immediately therefore I sent to thee (Peter); and thou
> hast well done that thou art come."—*Acts x*, 33.

The soldier-like praise for prompt obedience.

Asleep in Prison

> "The same night Peter was sleeping between two soldiers."
> —*Acts, xii*, 6.

In the garden Peter slept because his faith was weak—in
the prison he slept because his faith was strong. "He
giveth his beloved sleep."

Slogan or Benediction

"And when they had ordained them elders in every church, and had prayed with fasting, they commended them to the Lord."—*Acts xiv*, 23.

The world says, "Take care of yourself"; Christians say, "The Lord be with you."

A Godly Mother

"Timotheus, the son of a certain woman, which was a Jewess, and believed."—*Acts xvi*, 1.

Praise God for a godly mother.

His Hands Rest on Little Children

"That they should seek the Lord, if haply they might feel after him, and find him, though he be not far from every one of us."—*Acts xvii*, 27.

So near that all can touch. He came so low that His hands reached the heads of little children. Philosophy makes slow progress in saving men. It has eyes to see man's misery, but no hands to lift him out.

Proper Action

"And the rest, some on boards, and some on broken pieces of the ship. And so it came to pass, that they escaped all safe to land."—*Acts xxvii*, 44.

Use all legitimate means and trust in God. Splendid, when we reach the heavenly shore.

Melting an Enemy

"Thou shalt heap coals of fire on his head."
—*Rom. xii*, 20.

Christians are to heap acts of kindness on the head of an enemy, and so melt down his obstinacy, and overcome his evil by their good.

All Things to All Men

"I am made all things to all men."—1 *Cor. ix*, 22.

He would transgress no laws to please men, yet he would accommodate himself to all men where he could do it lawfully.

Absent—Present

"We are confident, I say, and willing rather to be absent from the body, and to be present with the Lord."—2 *Cor. v*, 8.

Paul did not believe in Purgatory evidently, nor in sleep before resurrection.

An Unchanging Law

"Whatsoever a man soweth, that shall he also reap."
—*Gal. vi*, 7.

The thing reaped is the thing sown, only multiplied one hundred times. Every man his own outgrowth.

CHAPTER III

"GIVE me these too, dear Lord," is the comment engraved in the Bishop's Bible against the verse, "And God gave Solomon wisdom and understanding exceeding much, and largeness of heart." Is this, in part, the secret of his fund of sagacious sayings, his wisdom, his swift shafts of wit, his largeness of heart, his understanding and deep human sympathy, his influence and winsomeness, and his naturalness and serene poise, his simple yet penetrating sayings?

Keeping Promises

Those who are conscientious in keeping promises are careful in making them.

Noah's Carpenters

"And Noah only remained alive, and they that were with him in the ark."—*Gen. vii*, 23.

Do you know what became of Noah's carpenters? They climbed up some other way rather than enter by the only door, and were lost.

Creation

We cannot explain the existence of a man or fly without God.

The Heavenly Dove

"And the dove came in to him in the evening, and lo, in her mouth was an olive leaf pluckt off."—*Gen. viii*, 11.

The Holy Spirit, the Heavenly Dove, brings the olive leaf of assurance from a new Heaven and earth—the former passed away.

Nebuchadnezzar

"I beheld till the wings thereof were plucked."
                                    —*Dan. vii*, 4.

Wings plucked, somewhat clucked !

True Singing

"Then sang Moses and the children of Israel. . . . The Lord is my strength and my song."—*Exod. xv*, 1, 2.

Not until we *see* can we *sing*. It is when we consider Him that the song is easily acquired. Arabs might have joined in the notes and words but not in the song. Though redeemed, sorrow and sighing had blinded Israel's eyes and kept back the song. Let us watch and pray against changing our song into discontent.

A Change of Method

"It repenteth me that I have set up Saul to be King. . . . And it grievèd Samuel and he cried unto the Lord all night."
                                    —*1 Sam. xv*, 11.

God's word and dealings with the wicked cause all good men to pray. God's repentance is not a change of mind but of method.

A Devout Prayer

"And God gave Solomon wisdom and understanding exceeding much, and largeness of heart, even as the sand that is on the sea shore."—1 *Kings iv*, 29.

Give me these too, dear Lord.

Sweetening Bitter Waters

"And he went forth unto the spring of the waters and cast the salt in there, and said, Thus saith the Lord, I have healed these waters."—2 *Kings ii*, 21.

A picture of our life work. Shall we try and sweeten bitter springs? Jesus did.

The Benediction of a good man's presence

"And Elisha said, As the Lord of hosts liveth, before whom I stand, surely were it not that I regard the presence of Jehoshaphat the king of Judah, I would not look toward thee nor see thee."—2 *Kings iii*, 14.

How often is a man blessed through a Christian's company.

Difficulties are Opportunities

"These are they that went over Jordan in the first month, when it had over-flown all his banks."—1 *Chron. xii*, 15.

Difficulties are only opportunities to strong men to manifest their strength.

Pedigrees Required

"These sought their register among those that were reckoned by genealogy, but they were not found."—*Ezra ii*, 62.

No priests will be permitted in Heaven unless they can prove their pedigree.

A Good Collection

"They gave after their ability unto the treasure of the work, three score and one thousand drams of gold and five thousand pound of silver, and one hundred priests' garments."
—*Ezra ii*, 69.

A good collection from a willing people, considering theirs was a land without commerce and they were in difficulties.

To Transform the Countenance

"Wherefore the king said unto me, Why is thy countenance sad, seeing thou art not sick ? This is nothing else but sorrow of heart."—*Neh. ii*, 2.

We may have salvation from a sad countenance—If God be for us, who can be against us ?

Man—A Worshipper

"In that day a man shall cast his idols of silver and his idols of gold, which they made each one for himself to worship, to the moles and to the bats."—*Isa. ii*, 20.

Man is a worshipping animal. His face is upward unlike the beasts.

Resolutions

Resolutions are like railway carriages without an engine. Actions (Engines) are wanted.

Two Sorts of Temptations

Whilst the Devil tempts to fall, God tempts to try.

A Vital Distinction

We may know the life of Christ, but do we know Christ the Life ?

Ezekiel and Daniel

Were it not for Ezekiel in Chebar and Daniel in Babylon, the captivity would have been almost a blank in the history of the Jews.

A Wife in the Will of God

"And Jacob fled into the country, and Israel served for a wife, and for a wife he kept sheep."—*Hos. xii*, 12.

Although 77, Jacob would rather *serve long*, for a wife in accordance with God's will and his father's wishes, than take a wife of other nations and be helped by them.

A Plumbline

"Behold, I will set a plumbline in the midst of my people Israel."—*Amos vii*, 8.

What is crooked, make Thou straight; what is not upright, Lord make right.

Love Never Faileth

1 Corinthians xiii. What *love* here does, Christ who came to manifest God the Father, *did*—hence God is love. There are five great gifts which are prized and honoured in the Church, but without love they are worthless. 1. Eloquence. 2. Theology. 3. Faith (enthusiastic). 4. Liberality. 5. Zeal. Thus where love is not, Christianity is not, and the converse is true as St. John teaches— Where love is, Christian is—for love never faileth.

Glory and Duty Connected

"I therefore, the prisoner of the Lord, beseech you that ye walk worthy of the vocation wherewith ye are called."
—*Eph. iv*, 1.

What a transition from the lofty account of the present glory and infinite hopes of the Church to these exhortations, but Paul ever connected faith and righteousness— the obligations of human duty with the revelations of Divine love. When we are conscious of possessing no merit, then we shall be conscious of suffering no injustice, even in darkest hours.

Lifelong Training

"But if ye be without chastisement, whereof all are partakers, then are ye bastards and not sons."—*Heb. xii*, 8.

Let us pity the poor unchastened ones. God's training lasts as long as there is room for growth in holiness, hence until death.

The Sixth Sense

By five senses the visible world comes before us; by the sixth, or faith (a new eye), the invisible world comes before us.

The Best Market

"I counsel thee to buy of me gold tried in the fire that thou mayest be rich."—*Rev. iii*, 18.

In buying at this market, we part with nothing valuable— sin, self-confidence.